WHY
SOLANGE
MATTERS

Music
Matters

Evelyn McDonnell and Oliver Wang

Series Editors

BOOKS IN THE SERIES

Tanya Pearson, *Why Marianne Faithfull Matters*
Charles L. Hughes, *Why Bushwick Bill Matters*
Adele Bertei, *Why Labelle Matters*
Fred Goodman, *Why Lhasa de Sela Matters*
Karen Tongson, *Why Karen Carpenter Matters*
Tom Smucker, *Why the Beach Boys Matter*
Donna Gaines, *Why the Ramones Matter*

WHY SOLANGE MATTERS

Stephanie Phillips

UNIVERSITY OF TEXAS PRESS
AUSTIN

Requests for permission to reproduce material from this work should be sent to:
  Permissions
  University of Texas Press
  P.O. Box 7819
  Austin, TX 78713-7819
  utpress.utexas.edu/rp-form

♾ The paper used in this book meets the minimum requirements of ANSI/NISO
Z39.48-1992 (R1997) (Permanence of Paper).

Library of Congress Cataloging-in-Publication Data
Names: Phillips, Stephanie (Music journalist) author.
Title: Why Solange matters / Stephanie Phillips.
Other titles: Music matters.
Description: First edition. | Austin: University of Texas Press, 2021. | Series: Music
matters | Includes bibliographical references.
Identifiers: LCCN 2020030547 (print) | LCCN 2020030548 (ebook)
  ISBN 978-1-4773-2008-2 (paperback)
  ISBN 978-1-4773-2249-9 (ebook other)
  ISBN 978-1-4773-2250-5 (ebook)
Subjects: LCSH: Solange, 1986– | African American women singers—Biography. |
African American singers—Biography. | Women singers—United States—Biography.
| Rhythm and blues musicians—Biography.
Classification: LCC ML420.S67957 P55 2021 (print) | LCC ML420.S67957 (ebook) |
DDC 7821.42164092 [B]—dc23
LC record available at https://lccn.loc.gov/2020030547
LC ebook record available at https://lccn.loc.gov/2020030548

doi:10.7560/320082

For all the revolutionary sistah punks out there.
Stay loud.

CONTENTS

Preface xi

1. Solange Takes Her Seat 1

2. Little Sister...25

3. The Making of a Solo Star...49

4. Bite the Hand, It Never Fed You................................75

5. Rooting for Everybody Black 103

6. Creating Community...129

7. For Us, By Us 161

8. When I Get Home...179

Epilogue...205

Acknowledgments..213

Notes...217

PREFACE

Solange both should and shouldn't be, which is what fascinates me about her. As the sister to a successful pop star and daughter of a self-taught business manager who catapulted that sister to the top, Solange was always going to be in the limelight. What has not been as predictable is how she carved out her space in the world: choosing to prioritize her independence and seek out new disciplines to develop her creativity, all while reclaiming and discarding various identities until she could finally put together an amalgamation of them all that suited her.

Her need to be seen as an individual unconnected to the accomplishments of others was finally achieved with the release of *A Seat at the Table* in 2016. The album was her ode to Black culture, Black feminism, her elders, as well as a document of the impact of racism and ancestral trauma on Black people's mental well-being. *A Seat at the Table* managed to accomplish the near-impossible feat of creating political art that is important in its own right, beyond the message it carries—a misstep that has led many cultural figures astray over the years. Her profound examinations of Blackness were part of a larger movement of Black creatives at the time (including Kendrick Lamar, Frank Ocean, Janelle Monáe, D'Angelo, and her sister Beyoncé). These artists created work that allows for a greater understanding of the concerns, pain, and grievances of the Black community. Solange is another example of the increased appetite for socially conscious art that occurred post Black Lives Matter; she also reflects the gatekeeping that often shuts out people of color from alternative music scenes, the popularity of genre-bounding Black experimental artists, and the connections across the Black diaspora around the world. Her story is the link that joins a myriad of disparate threads to form part of the Black millennial identity.

I'm one of those Black millennials. I'm also a journalist and a musician based in London. I play in the Black feminist punk band Big Joanie, and I'm also part of a collective that organizes the London-based punk festival celebrating people of color, Decolonise Fest. Solange is someone who has been a part of my life for decades, even though at first I barely realized she was there. As a tweenage Destiny's Child fanatic growing up in the UK, I joined in the frenetic screaming and unprompted sing-alongs to every minute of their 2002 show at Birmingham's National Indoor Arena, oblivious to the fact that Solange accompanied the group as a backup dancer. As I grew in awareness of her work, Solange became both the first choice on my house party playlists and the medium through which I'd launder my emotions. Listening to *A Seat at the Table* gave me a space to better understand my own experiences of racism and the daily microaggressions I and other people of color experience. The album was an extension of the Black feminism I practiced in my daily life, through which I could feel pride in my approach to creating culture, developing connections with my own community, and communicating with the people I love. She gave me space to learn to love what I describe in various ways throughout the book as my Black girl weirdo self.

Though it may seem like Solange and I operate in different universes, I see my band, along with many other Black experimental musicians, as part of the same movement. It is a movement that seeks to delve into the expansiveness of Black art beyond the limited imagination of the white mainstream. It aims to create, removed from the gatekeepers of the cultural world, by setting up our own independent presses, event promotion collectives, publishers, and record labels. It is a movement that felt unconnected at first, with the many collectives and groups that arose around the world, one at a time, seemingly without knowledge of one another. To me, the peak of this movement erupted around the time of the resurgence in popularity of terms like "intersectionality," when Black feminist activist theory was democratically shared for anyone to access across social media in the early 2010s.

A Seat at the Table is a masterpiece in itself, but this book will not discuss one moment in this artist's career. Rather, through this book I hope to analyze the overarching themes found in Solange's work as well as her full transition from afterthought to the planet's biggest pop star to unconventional cultural icon, taking in every step she made along the way, not just because it led to *A Seat at the Table*, but because it documents her journey toward self-actualization and discovery. By analyzing her growth, I aim to show that her skill as a songwriter and a creative was apparent from an early age and that the unconventional journey she took toward pop stardom was essential to her becoming the artist we know today.

Solange's journey is nowhere near done. While I was writing this book, she released *When I Get Home*, a sparse, sonically soothing record that is a complete departure from *A Seat at the Table* and has forced music critics like me to reconsider who we believe Solange Knowles to be. She will continue to release, to confound and surprise us. Other books will be written about her, as well as this particular moment in music culture. For now, *Why Solange Matters* will focus on the cultural impact of Solange Knowles, to understand how her work and approaches are part of a wider cultural movement that has revolutionized a generation.

— 1 —

SOLANGE TAKES HER SEAT

On an evening in late September 2016, a Black southern mother did as many Black southern mothers do and cooked for her daughter. The nostalgic aroma of a homemade meal and the soothing calm of a maternal presence were desperately needed, as the moment her daughter had been planning for years was days, hours even, away. Her eldest daughter spent the week with her sister, offering reassurance and advice from her lengthy experience with nerves-inducing events such as these. Though the daughter was no stranger to this occasion, she found herself more anxious than she'd ever been, breaking out in hives and unable to sit still. It was a passion project that in many ways she was destined to create and had been working on for three years (right up to the point when she sent it off to her label mere days before the record was released). But she was worried she had exposed too much of herself in her music and was unsure how this would be interpreted. As the three women sat together in anticipation, counting down the hours, the true story of their ancestors, in all of its despair and glory, was primed to enter into popular culture. It was a story that would establish all three women as bastions of Black pride in contemporary Black culture.

The women in question were none other than Solange Knowles; her older sister, Beyoncé Knowles-Carter; and their mother, Tina Knowles-Lawson, united in solidarity for Solange as she prepared for the launch of her third album, *A Seat at the Table*, released in 2016. Knowing the heights Solange has now reached, I struggle to envision her feeling anything other than unwavering self-belief in her ability to devastate, educate, and enrich audiences with her work. At that point in her lengthy career, which started when she was a teenager, Solange had been on the receiving end of a litany of disparate critical takes. Her early releases were dismissed as tepid and uninspiring. Later, her music was acclaimed, but the praise for the work behind the scenes often fell on the men around her. Given her shaky history with the music industry, it is understandable that she would be unsure how her project focused on Black self-empowerment and healing would be received.

Fortunately, there was no need for concern. The release of the zeitgeist-shifting *A Seat at the Table* catapulted Solange into a new level of fame, gaining mainstream recognition for her artistry. The album landed on copious best-record-of-the-year lists, and Solange won a Grammy for Best R&B Performance for the song "Cranes in the Sky." It was a welcome relief from the negative energy surrounding the political climate of 2016, when the world was reeling from the lurch to the far right in Europe and awaiting the same in America with the rise of then presidential candidate Donald Trump. The twenty-one-track album of understated slow jams, stripped-back jazz, and deconstructed r&b is a sonic time capsule containing a mere fragment of the many strands that make up the Black experience for this generation. With southern storytelling tropes; New Orleans–inspired horns; Black British collaborators; conversations on trending topics of self-care, hair, and Black pride; and the inclusion of Black elders' voices, Solange captured her interpretation of the Black voice for listeners to turn up to eleven and sing along to (or cry with if they want) when needed most. Solange speaks directly to the Black community's complex relationship with pain, loss, healing, intergenerational trauma, ownership, and empowerment. It is a record that gains power from its lightness, owed to Solange's breathy falsetto, the lurching bass lines, the wandering jazz-influenced piano sections, and the polymathic drum beats that form the backbone of the instrumentals.

Writing for *Pitchfork*, Julianne Escobedo Shepherd captures the importance of the album: "Even though it's been out less than a week, it already seems like a document of historical significance, not just for its formidable musical achievements but for the way it encapsulates Black cultural and social history with such richness, generosity, and truth."[1] The historical significance of the album was almost predicted, both with the grandiosity of its own aims and by Solange's use of museums and exhibition spaces as venues on her tour. Through her singular vision and labor, Solange inducted her album into the vaults of history on her own terms.

A Seat at the Table set Solange free from outside expectations, allowing her to create 2019's *When I Get Home*. The album is an exploration of her hometown of Houston set to a soundtrack of New Age jazz chopped and screwed–inspired compositions, and thundering bass lines. The record's hazy ambivalence and free-form jazz approach, to my mind, make the album sound like a spaced-out continuous jam. It is an approach that can render the album directionless in nature and overtly cerebral to the wrong ears. Though it met with some mixed reviews, *When I Get Home* is perhaps as close to the musical embodiment of Solange as we may ever get. Where *A Seat at the Table* was her careful consideration of the Black female identity, *When I Get Home* saw her unrestrained from having to perform her trauma. She was free to do whatever she wanted, and what she wanted to do was fly her freak flag high and proud.

While promoting *When I Get Home*, Solange spoke of the joy she felt at not being confined by expectations "to give anything to anyone that was not a part of me in this present moment," adding, "Any time you truly feel seen, you feel a certain level of joy."[2] Seventeen years after her 2002 debut, she was finally able to inject herself into her art, creating an accurate depiction of herself at that moment in time.

Herein lies my fascination with Solange and the impetus I found to write this book. Her artistic and cultural significance is the result of more than just one or two albums. It is her journey and her self-determinism that granted her full artistic freedom. Solange has transformed from a teen pop star living out her Aaliyah fantasy under the shadow of her famous sister to a critically acclaimed powerhouse of Black feminist thought and musicianship. She worked through her struggles to find her identity and belonging in an often unforgiving industry, at every turn creating her own path and calling to others to accompany her on her journey. She became her own producer; started her own label; curated her own enviable, effortless sense of style; and chose to lead culture rather than meekly follow along. To watch Solange is to see a version of unapologetic Blackness many Black people aspire to—one that doesn't subscribe to previous notions of what it means to be Black, one aware of self-preservation, one that doesn't give a fuck about what Becky in the back thinks Black people should do.

Despite her success, she still elicits strong reactions, which makes her an even more intriguing figure. When I brought up my book to friends, family, and coworkers, I received one of two responses. For the majority of white people, a quizzical look would appear on their face. Solange? Are you sure you don't mean Beyoncé? What does Solange do, why would you write about her, why would she matter? Even the veteran music journalist Robert Christgau was unimpressed by *A Seat at the Table*: "I assume its rep [reputation] isn't just some mass delusion—that there's something there, and that it has to do with Black female identity. But it left me unmoved, indeed untouched, and I'm not gonna lie about it."[3] I appreciate that Christgau admitted his lived experience as a white man may have hindered the album's appeal for him, given its focus on Black womanhood.

Later, however, he said that as a "lyric-conscious African-American feminist," Solange should have been right up his alley.[4] At first, I found these two statements to be contradictory, until I realized the lyric-conscious Black feminist of Christgau's imagination has little to do with the thoughts or feelings of real Black women. Christgau, like many other white liberals, seemingly wanted a tame version of Black feminism that gave him access to Blackness without challenging his privilege. *A Seat at the Table* highlighted the conversations Black people have when white people aren't around, and at times directly called out the insidious nature of white privilege and racial stereotypes on songs like "Junie" and "Mad." The narrative of the album does not center whiteness; it allows listeners to come to terms with the reality of Black life as well as the horrors inflicted on Black people. It leaves the white liberal with no place to look away, so perhaps Christgau found the album hit too close to home.

Celebrity gossip media reacted similarly, exemplified by the website TMZ discussing Beyoncé and Solange and sneering that Solange's famous 2014 altercation with brother-in-law Jay-Z in an elevator was "her biggest hit" until *A Seat at the Table*.[5] Clearly, white people and the tabloids saw Solange as a flash-in-the-pan pop star who made little impact on their daily lives.

In contrast, Black people's reaction to the book idea was a knowing nod, followed by an emphatic grin as a glazed look of wonder crossed their faces. I can only assume they were daydreaming about what Solange meant to them. Prior to *A Seat at the Table*, Solange's status as a Knowles; her up-tempo r&b hits; and daring, kaleidoscopic wardrobe made her a favorite among a particular brand of Black millennials who love to see Black women winning. She was outspoken when it came to calling out prejudice in the music industry and systemic police violence and demonstrating her love for Black culture. One of my favorite examples took place at the 2018 Met Gala, where, to pay homage to the theme of the night, "Heavenly Bodies: Fashion and the Catholic Imagination," Solange walked the red carpet in a black PVC dress, leather boots, a halo of blond braids, and a flowing black durag. In gold Gothic type on the hem of the garment in question were the words "My God Wears a Durag." It was a conceptually high-fashion moment that revered an otherwise everyday item in Black households.

A Seat at the Table's confessional and melancholic exploration of Black life in the United States gave many in the Black community—wherever they lived—a chance to see their lives reflected back to them through a medium and persona they connected with. Solange's work is so often referenced that it has become part of the Black diaspora's ever-growing lingo, popping up in Twitter in-jokes and shareable memes. She has morphed into Arthur mash-up memes and extended Twitter threads where Kermit the Frog acts out every single action in "Cranes in the Sky." For Lakeisha Goedluck, a Black British journalist who first reviewed the album for the independent music and culture publication *Crack Magazine*, songs like "Don't Touch My Hair" resonated deeply: "Solange's voice is very melodic, calm. But I think the imperative nature of the song and the many times I felt that way made it the most instantly relatable. Out of my friends who are women of colour, that was the song that most of them messaged me about, like, 'Oh my god, have you heard Solange's album? "Don't Touch My Hair" is a bop.'"[6]

Hearing topics that often arise in conversations with friends documented so lovingly makes listening to Solange a communal experience. In *A Seat at the Table*, I hear the roaring belly laughs of my friends, the consistently prescient advice of my elders, and my own inner monologue reminding myself to just do what I need to do. I spoke to the Brooklyn-based digital journalist Natelegé Whaley about watching Solange at the annual music and culture event Essence Festival, in a predominantly Black female crowd. Whaley told me: "I'm sitting there watching her, and I'm about to cry, as if I hadn't heard these songs so many times prior to going to the festival. It reminds you of soul-stirring gospel music or soul-stirring r&b that just hits you in this place where you just like, 'Ah, man, I gotta let this go. I gotta let these tears flow out.' It's like healing. And I think, once again, I don't know how exactly she did it, but she made it, and I think all that authenticity shines through."[7]

In many ways it is correct to say Solange's authenticity comes from the evolution she went through to become the person she is today. Her search for self is deeply relatable. I understand the need to prove oneself, to try out different versions of yourself in the hope you'll be accepted, only to be met with doubt and confusion. Her path toward self-acceptance, following her natural hair journey, and her candid conversations about identity mirrored the path I and many of my friends took to free ourselves from the white-centric worldview that composes mainstream society in the UK. For myself and many other Black women, we root so hard for Solange because we see ourselves in her and don't want her to fail, just as we don't want ourselves to fail.

SMALL ISLAND LIFE

Back in 2016, my life held little similarity with the trend-setting existence Solange led. I was sharing a room in a South London multi-occupant flat with my then boyfriend, coping with infestations of mice or clothes moths like many who live at the whims of the floundering London housing market, and dealing with my passive-aggressive boss at my dead-end content writing job. As in any bustling international city, life in London is simultaneously the entry point to realizing all of your dreams and a waking nightmare composed of overpriced coffee and men who wear teeny-tiny beanie hats and grubby clothes to disguise the fact that Mummy and Daddy provide them with a monthly allowance.

Though London is the political, cultural, and business hub of the country and the city most people have in their minds when they think about Britain, if you're looking for the quintessentially British experience, London is the wrong place to find it. Within this small collection of islands known for passive aggression, a masochistic addiction to worshiping the upper classes, and light rain that soaks you right through, London, culturally, is almost a floating separate state. If you want to experience the real England, you need to leave the M25 motorway that borders the city and venture out to the rest of the country. In my opinion, the area that best represents the UK is my hometown, Wolverhampton. If you haven't heard of Wolverhampton before, don't worry, there's little reason for that name to ring a bell. Wolverhampton is a small, working-class former industrial city in the middle of England. Like many former industrial areas, the city has a strong South Asian and Caribbean community. Both came from former British colonies in their thousands on request from the British government to help prop up the country, after it was decimated by World War II, and became the doctors, nurses, and health administrators who were the foundations of our National Health Service.

Wolverhampton is not really a city, just a large town. In the UK, a place was considered a city only if there was a cathedral. In 2000, to celebrate a new millennium and Y2K not bringing about the end of the world, the government decided to bestow city status onto a handful of towns of their choosing. Wolverhampton, along with Inverness in Scotland and Brighton and Hove on the southeast coast, were selected to became representations of the new world that Prime Minister Tony Blair, leader of the Labour Party, wanted the UK to move toward. The New Labour government, as it was colloquially known because of its dramatic shift away from the overtly socialist concerns of previous Labour governments, prioritized social mobility. The Millennium Cities Initiative (MCI) was a large-scale attempt at tackling social mobility, because the working classes had been so demonized in the media and politics. It literally tried to make a whole town upwardly mobile. Very little positive change happened for the city. Our main industries and factories have died, and the shopping centers have become ghost towns full of boarded-up shop fronts, but our people stayed the same.

I should probably take some time to quickly explain the class structure in the UK, as its constituent parts differ greatly from those in the United States and the rest of the world. The class structure that dominates British society is one of the most defining aspects of our culture. Class is distinguished as much, or sometimes even more, by our culture, actions, and family history as by how much money we make. Working in the service industry or in low-paid jobs indicates you are working class as much as the fact that you might be able to afford one budget resort holiday a year and don't have time to visit museums. Conversely, a middle-class person is as easily spotted by their middle management job as they are by their access to and display of knowledge in their towering bookcases and too-big-for-the-city 4x4 Range Rovers. In the 1990s, the UK was obsessed with becoming middle class.

I grew up at the height of this period, in the 1990s and early 2000s, taking in this warped rhetoric through my generation's fixation with university, a tactic that left us overqualified, saddled with debt, and, once the 2008 recession hit, with no jobs or straightforward career path to follow. The allure of bettering oneself through education was natural for the child of Jamaican immigrants who reminded my brother and me that this country would give us nothing for free, so we had to take what we could, equip ourselves with the knowledge and tools to succeed, and never allow work to take over our lives. This early education in resistance and self-reliance was born of my family's experiences living in a country where racism and discrimination were the insidious roots of everyday life. My parents worked hard to practice what they preached and achieved the Caribbean dream of homeownership and lower-level office jobs. My dad worked in the accounts department for a local factory, my mum as a secretary in a local administrative branch of the NHS; together they embodied English lower-middle-class aspiration.

In that lower-middle-class home was my dad's unwieldy

collection of reggae, which was all ripped CDs in jewel cases with home-printed album covers. Though he had a tendency to play them loudly on a Saturday night, it is the only loud thing about him. Otherwise he is a mild-mannered, thoughtful person who was happy as long as he could go to the pub on Fridays and watch the football. My mum is similarly composed, but also quietly revolutionary in everything she does. To me, she represents the straightforward way many working-class people and people of color practice their politics on a daily basis. She was a strong Labour Party supporter and explained to me as a child why they were the best hope for working people in this country. She believed that you should always do right by your own conscience, and talked constantly to me and my brother about Black history. My confidence in my Blackness remained strong inside my own home; it was only when I left and encountered a world that told me the opposite of what my parents taught that I began to feel confused. I attended majority white schools throughout my childhood, despite Wolverhampton having a large Caribbean and South Asian community. Rarely seeing depictions of beauty that looked like me, and hanging out with friends who made casual jokes about my race while declaring that everyone is equal felt like I spent much of my school life being gaslit. This was on top of the fact that as a shy, clumsy, reserved girl, I was always going to be unpopular anyway.

When I turned fifteen, I was drawn to music beyond

the pop and r&b of acts like Destiny's Child, TLC, and Kelis that I still loved, to include music that reflected the way I felt inside; I became an emo. I picked up a cheap black eyeliner from the market, bought a tacky studded belt, attempted to swoop my chemically relaxed hair into a side fringe despite the obvious indications it wasn't going to work, and went for it. I listened to the Welsh post-hardcore band Funeral for a Friend on my portable Discman on the bus to school every day for months. I became a devoted follower of the Yeah Yeah Yeahs, Bikini Kill, Sleater-Kinney, the White Stripes, the Distillers, and so many British indie bands. My mum, witnessing my love for music, and taking the many hints I gave her, bought me a Yamaha acoustic guitar for my sixteenth birthday, which I immediately used to play power chord–heavy feminist punk. When I listened to my favorite artists, sometimes I closed my eyes and put my hand on my chest. I could feel the lyrics pounding in my throat, the words rushing to get out, but I didn't know how to release them. I knew music was a part of me, but becoming one with it seemed impossible. The music I loved was varied and, to my mind, reflected who I was; other people disagreed. As an embarrassingly shy Black girl with thick glasses who regularly listened to overly sincere emo and alternative bands, I was often told by both Black and white friends that I wasn't like other Black people. The line was sometimes meant as a compliment, sometimes not. Nevertheless, it riled me every time. Didn't they see I loved my Blackness as much as anyone else, that I was taught to never forget the brutal history of British colonialism that led my people to this rainy, overcast island, that I learned everyday activism from my mum who boycotted racist institutions like the *Sun* newspaper, owned by the media magnate Rupert Murdoch. I knew I wasn't any different from other Black people, I just needed to find a place where numerous visions of Blackness were allowed to exist.

In 2006, when I was eighteen, I said good-bye to Wolverhampton and moved to southwest England to study journalism and English literature at Kingston University. After I graduated, I moved to the big city of London, setting up a home in Brixton, South London. The area is synonymous with the Black British community. It has been home to the activist Olive Morris, the fiery heart of Black British rebellion during the Brixton riots, and the stomping grounds of the proto–riot grrrl punk icon Poly Styrene. My determination to find places where my Blackness could exist sparked the formation of my Black feminist punk band, Big Joanie. It was why I joined a feminist consciousness-raising group for women of color, why I brought a group of plucky punks of color together to start our own festival celebrating the legacy of people of color in the punk scene—Decolonise Fest. It is the same spirit that led me to Solange.

The first time I heard Solange's voice wasn't on one of her own songs but on a cover of Dirty Projectors' "Stillness Is the Move," self-released DIY style in 2009. I didn't think much of Dirty Projectors prior to that, but once her version came out, I couldn't get it out of my head. I fell in love with her wispy vocals and her defiant love for indie rock. Solange's take on "Stillness Is the Move" brought even more Black culture into a song that already heavily referenced elements of r&b history. The sampling of Soul Mann and the Brothers' "Bumpy's Lament" and her choice to take the song up an octave in those closing final bars felt like a welcome passive-aggressive nod to the white indie rock scene that took everything from Black culture but Black people (I will delve deeper into this topic in chapter 4). I was ready to show my allegiance to the one true Solange, but beyond a couple of late-night dance sessions to "Losing You" from 2012's *True* EP, that moment didn't show itself until *A Seat at the Table*.

I was lying in bed on my day off, sluggishly trying to muster the energy to focus on anything productive. It was mid-morning on an unusually sunny September day when my friend Chardine Taylor-Stone, a cultural activist and drummer in my band Big Joanie, messaged me. I had to listen to Solange's new album, and I had to do it now. Ever since I first met her at a Black feminist meeting in 2013, when she decided we should stay in touch because I was carrying a tote bag with British post-punk pioneers "The Raincoats" plastered on the front, Chardine has always possessed an unbeatable track record when it comes to music taste. So if she said Solange was where I should be, that was exactly where I went.

I listened to the album from start to finish, then started over again. I stared in awe at the beauty on display in her videos, Black people drenched in heavenly garments I could only dream of putting together. *A Seat at the Table* felt like it was written specifically for me. I imagined Solange reaching out from the screen and serenading me in my dingy bedroom, staring deep into my eyes. In that moment, in my head, Solange went from proprietor of sweet upbeat jams to the creator of head-turning anthems that gave my Black girl weirdo self a space to exhale. It was a version of the expansive Blackness I moved cities for and, in many ways, tried to create in my own punk scene. Her determination to make everything on her own terms was appealing to me as a musician who started out in the DIY punk scene, which prides itself on working with your community to create the world you want to see. That she continually referred to the record as her "punk" album, because she believed it was her time to "shake things up and be loud," only endeared her even more to me.[8] And though the album spoke specifically to African American issues, it was still a welcome salve to the historically downtrodden Black British community.

Three months before *A Seat at the Table* was released, the UK voted to leave the European Union. The referendum vote was a culmination of years of rising Islamophobia and racism, ever-present xenophobia, and the inability of the British public to conceive that the country was changing. In the aftermath of "Brexit," as the referendum came to be known, hate crime rose sharply, with government statistics showing figures in England and Wales that were 44 percent higher in July 2016 compared to the previous year.[9] Much was made of the age and class division in the Brexit vote, but the racial division was just as eye opening: 73 percent of Black voters and 67 percent of Asian voters voted to remain, compared to 53 percent of white voters who chose to leave.[10] The stark difference in voting habits showed people of color were more attuned to the prejudices surrounding the rhetoric of the referendum. One of the many grim outcomes from Brexit is that it allowed the country to once again show its true face to its Black and Brown inhabitants, many of whom are only here because of British colonial rule.

Britain is seen by the world, and in turn prefers to see itself, as the benevolent face of colonialism: a fair and balanced power that looks after its subjects and wouldn't dream of committing the brutal acts of racism seen in the United States. In England we shake our heads, looking down on the United States, patting ourselves on the back for a job well done at creating a thriving multicultural society in which meritocracy rules. Of course, this vision is just a dream cooked up by the English white elite to avoid dealing with reality. Institutional racism is the decaying cornerstone of British society; the scars are easy to see if you're willing to look. Our policing is no better than that in America; following the racist murder of Black British teenager Stephen Lawrence in 1993, the Metropolitan Police were found to be institutionally racist and incompetent in their handling of the case. When Black people die in police custody in England, we still get no justice (Sean Rigg, Sheku Bayoh, and Sarah Reed are just a few of the victims); our communities are overpoliced (the shooting of Dorothy "Cherry" Groce during a violent police raid of her home sparked the 1985 Brixton riot); and 51 percent of boys in young offender institutions (prisons for young people aged 15-21) are identified as being from an ethnic minority background.[11] Elsewhere in UK society, Black and ethnic minority groups are twice as likely to live in poverty as white people;[12] the highest rungs of political, financial, and cultural power are reserved for the white upper classes; our media is littered with racism and xenophobia; and up until 2015, British taxpayer money was used to compensate slave owners following the 1833 Slavery Abolition Act.

The Windrush generation, Caribbean migrants who came to the country from former British colonies between the 1940s and the 1970s, are often lauded for their hard work and can-do spirit, but they were victims of a heart-wrenchingly cruel scandal. In 2018, it was revealed that Commonwealth nationals living in the UK were being wrongly threatened with deportation and denied legal rights. There were at least eighty-three cases in which people were incorrectly deported. Despite all coming from nations that were under British rule, in 2012 when immigration law changed, people were told to prove continuous residence in the UK going back to 1973 in order to work legally, claim benefits, or access healthcare. It was difficult to prove, as few kept records going back that far, and the landing cards of Windrush migrants, which would show they were here legally, were destroyed by the Home Office in 2010. The fallout from this led to many elderly people being deported to countries they had not seen for years, losing their jobs, and being denied medical care because they couldn't prove their citizenship. To add further pain, at least eleven people wrongly deported from the UK have died, and many have died in the UK—like fifty-eight-year-old Dexter Bristol, who died of heart problems—while trying to prove their citizenship. Younger generations have also suffered, as those whose parents could not prove their citizenship or were born outside the UK and raised here also had their identity questioned and were threatened with deportation. This has resulted in convicted offenders being deported to countries they've never known, no matter how small the crime, leaving many to feel they were being doubly punished.

This is the true history of England; one that is brutal and conniving, but rarely acknowledged. To those outside of these islands we may look like a timid group, but in reality, British racism lies within every aspect of our society. It is the same brand of racism that Solange speaks out against on *A Seat at the Table*, one that connects the Black diaspora and unites us in our shared experience. This is why *A Seat at the Table* was so powerful to me and other Black Brits. The world of *A Seat at the Table* allowed Black people to derive power from our community, reminding us that we can exist and thrive beyond external expectations. In a society that only wants to exclude, pass judgment, and stereotype, *A*

Seat at the Table gave the Black community permission to envision a world beyond the negative one we were in. I took *A Seat at the Table* to my terrible job and let "Mad," a song about Black rage, get me through quasi-racist conversations and awkward interactions with colleagues. It seeped into my personal life, becoming a shorthand reference between me and my Black female friends. It made me confident in my choice to surround myself with strong Black women and develop a Black feminist socialist outlook that strives for a better future for the Black community and all oppressed people.

POCKETS OF BLACK GIRLS

My connection to Solange grew even deeper when I saw her live at London's Lovebox festival in 2017. Despite having barely any money, I didn't hesitate to buy tickets. I followed her sparse touring schedule and realized it was probably my only chance to see her live. So my friends and I headed out to Victoria Park in East London with baby's breath flowers in our hair; glitter on our faces; and a built-up resolve to deal with blotchy-faced, irritating eighteen-year-olds who, without fail, manage to get blind drunk by 2 p.m. and stagger around threatening to vomit in the festival toilets. This was all done in the name of Solange. Our friendship group had almost exhausted our conversations around Solange. What would she be like? What if she doesn't live up to the hype? What will she be wearing? It was time to see her in the flesh.

It was an unusually warm day for London, and the park was full of music lovers, teens enjoying their first festival experience, and posh bankers' kids looking for somewhere to keep the party going. We arrived early and wove our way through the crowd to get as close as we could to the stage until we reached two very tall white guys in front of us who were taking up a lot of space. My five-foot-three self could just about see the stage when I jumped and stood on tiptoes. The all-white stage props and towering circular backdrop that I recognized from online videos of her shows were in place, backlit by an orange-reddish glow. Maybe it was the overpriced wine or the low-key heatstroke we were all most likely suffering from, but we decided to talk about these men, loudly, right behind them. Shouts of "white supremacy" and "This is what she was talking about, boo" leaped from our mouths because we wanted to get closer. They seemed unfazed at first by our behavior, which was drunkenly petty, but we felt we had a right to do this. Solange was here to see *us*, so *we* needed to see her.

Eventually, Solange and her band walked out, dressed in a uniform of orange and red to roaring applause. From the opening bar of the first number, the crowd sang in unison. We all swayed along and forgot our jokey disagreement with the men in front of us. We grabbed each other, recited every lyric, and lived in the power of each word. Every millisecond of the band's performance was deliberate, from an on-beat shrug of the shoulders to the soft two-step sway of her horn section and guitarists. In a reworked intro to "Mad," Solange and her backup singers, with just a piano to accompany them, softly reminded us with the lyrics we've always needed, "You've got a right to be mad," ending on a gut-wrenching, discordant punk-rock scream that ripped through the crowd. It was one of many emotional moments in the set where Solange also revealed that she broke out of the hospital after being in for three days following a serious episode (she was battling an autonomic disorder, an experience she would go on to reveal later that year). Despite being told she couldn't perform, she came out telling us, "I knew this place was going to be filled with so much love."[13]

It was so emotional, the two men standing in front of us turned around with tears in their eyes. They were moved and wanted to share with us. Without words, one of them lifted me on his shoulders above the crowd, and suddenly I was in the air watching over everything. Solange was getting down to "F.U.B.U.," reminding the crowd that this was for all the Black people watching. Up there in the air, looking down from above on the sea of festival goers, I could suddenly see my place in this fandom. Throughout the crowd there were replicas of my own friendship group. Pockets of Black girls grouped together screaming and living in the moment. I turned my attention back to the stage, and Solange was standing directly in front of me, reaching out. I reached out to her. In my mind, she could see me. In my mind, I almost touched her.

– 2 –

LITTLE SISTER

Tucked away on an unassuming road in the upper-middle-class section of Third Ward, a predominantly African American area in Houston, Texas, was the house that would change Black culture forever. The Knowles home on Parkwood Drive was full of love, laughter, and talent. Parents Tina and Mathew Knowles were living the dream of Black empowerment; they came from relatively little and were determined to make more for themselves and their children.

Mathew was born in 1952 in Gadsden, Alabama. He was one of the first children in his area to integrate the school system. Facing vitriolic racism on a daily basis deeply affected him well into his later years, as Solange would discover while making *A Seat at the Table*. As a child of the generation that saw education and economic success as the ticket to freedom, Mathew took his studies seriously. He went to the historically Black college Fisk University, graduating in 1974, and eventually moved to Houston in 1976, where he became a successful businessman selling medical and office supplies, making a six-figure salary.

Tina Knowles (now Tina Lawson after the couple final-
ized their divorce in 2011 and Tina married the actor Rich-
ard Lawson in 2015) was born Célestine Ann Beyoncé in
Galveston, Texas, in 1954, the youngest of seven children.
She started her career as a makeup artist for the Japanese
cosmetics company Shiseido at age nineteen in California,
but left to look after her parents when they fell ill. After
the couple's marriage in 1980 and the birth of their eldest
daughter, Beyoncé, in 1981, they moved to the neighborhood where Solange grew up, surrounded by the families
of Black judges and doctors. Tina opened a twelve-seat hair
salon, Headliners, in Houston—a business that ran for two
decades. The family's already full house grew during the
mid-1990s when the Knowles family took in their friend
Kelly Rowland and the girls' first cousin Angela Beyincé
(who would contribute her songwriting skills to Beyoncé
and Destiny's Child as well as work at Beyoncé's company,
Parkwood Entertainment).

The family's wealthy lifestyle allowed the couple to
give their children everything they needed to succeed. On
his and Tina's doting approach to parenthood, Mathew
Knowles has said: "We paid a lot of attention to what our
kids' dreams were. Entertainment was a thing that they
loved and singing, so we focused on making sure they had
dance lessons and vocal lessons and things that they needed
and they wanted to do."[1] The Knowles family probably
had a packed schedule that would make most parents weep
in fear, but their dedication to their kids' creative talents

paid off sooner than they may have imagined. Along with the banging doors, pitched laughter, and blaring TV sets usually associated with a house full of children, they heard the stomp and clatter of newly learned dance steps and the unrefined vocals of three young girls who would later entertain millions.

SCHOOL DAZE

Solange Piaget Knowles was born on June 24, 1986, in Houston, Texas. From an early age, she established herself as the outspoken one in the family, a trait both she and her family believe stems from attempts to be heard over a house full of people, two of which were best friends and in a band together. She told *W* magazine in 2017: "Looking back, I hear these stories that even at two I was doing the most. But I do think that part of that was me trying to communicate and carve out a way to be heard."[2]

She spoke her mind outside her home, too, even when it landed her in trouble. She went to an all-Black school until the third grade, when she transferred to a predominantly white Christian school. Her school transfer could have been the result of her parents wanting to introduce her to the white America she had yet to experience. It may have been because it was a better school and worth the impact that a potentially hostile environment could have on her. Either way, according to Solange, the culture clash she experienced at her new school was "mind shattering."[3] In junior high, she was suspended from her strict Christian school after she refused to take down a topless poster of New York rapper Nas in her locker, deemed blasphemous due to his God's Son tattoo that provocatively straddled his midriff. Solange stood up to her dean, arguing that another student had a poster of Justin Timberlake, who had a cross tattoo, so she should be able to keep her poster, too. Her parents, who admired her ability to stand up for herself and couldn't argue with her position, told her to fight for what she believed in. She was given the choice to take down the poster or leave it up and get a suspension; she took the suspension on principle. Such confidence from a Black girl bothered some of her classmates, who referred to her as a "crazy, ugly, attention-seeking, weirdo."[4]

What others saw as attention seeking was a creativity and mode of self-expression that became a part of her life at an early age. She loved fashion, rocking up to school in a fur coat and cowboy boots, ignoring the stifled giggles and whispered remarks of her classmates. She took the same passion for curating her wardrobe and channeled it into the rest of her life, living in a constant cycle of creation. When she was ten years old, she wrote a poem about her Black ancestry and performed a version of the song "Strange Fruit" at a talent show. She would become obsessed with alt-rock singer-songwriter Alanis Morissette one week, and the five-octave range of soul soprano Minnie Riperton the next. Every now and again she would lock herself away in her bedroom with a drum kit, determined to write songs like her heroes.

That was one of many phases she went through during her adolescence. They include her Goth phase, spent moshing in the pit at Armenian American heavy metal group System of a Down gigs; her fixation with the art of dance; a bible-thumping phase; her phase as the club president of a group dedicated to celebrated singer-songwriter Fiona Apple; a Rastafari vegan phase; the football player's girlfriend phase; and, obviously, her Nas aficionado phase. In a revealing letter to her teenage self, published in *Teen Vogue* in 2017, Solange, like many young teens, was searching for her true identity, but she explained that those phases, no matter how short-lived, stayed with her: "you will sow each of these chapters in the land that you become. you will see bits and pieces of them scattered into the skin you grow into."[5] Looking back, it's easy to see how each one of these phases is still exhibited in Solange's personality and work today. The raw emotional tenderness of Fiona Apple is reflected in *True*, her exploration of relationship breakdowns. The exhilarating feeling of exorcising demons in a mosh pit has been replaced by the considered reflections and acceptance of anger on her "punk" album, *A Seat at the Table*.

One of her earliest childhood influences was the 1978 film *The Wiz*, an all-Black-led interpretation of *The Wizard of Oz* with Diana Ross in the lead role. The cult film stood out as one of the earliest examples of Black representation that young Solange could relate to. As a child, she performed in a community version of *The Wiz*, playing Glinda the Good Witch, a role made famous by the actress Lena Horne. "That was one of the first times I had a clear vision of how to use and emote these other parts of myself when I couldn't do dance or I couldn't do music."[6] *The Wiz* forced Solange to think of herself as a performer, and it continued to be a touchstone throughout her life, becoming the inspiration for the film accompanying her 2019 album, *When I Get Home*.

Her first love, mode of expression, and obsession, though, was dance. She spent her summers from the age of five to thirteen in a dance studio and dreamed of attending Juilliard. She saw herself in the Third Ward native Debbie Allen, who played dance teacher Lydia Grant on the musical drama TV series *Fame*. Solange became further entranced as a teenager when she watched Lauren Anderson, one of the first Black ballerinas to become a principal dancer in a major company, perform at the Houston Ballet. After a Destiny's Child backup dancer became pregnant, a thirteen-year-old Solange was asked to fill in for the summer tour. It was a trip that would open her eyes to Japanese culture, expose her to European pop stars like Björk and the Chemical Brothers, and give her the space and safety to explore the world as a young girl. She was so determined to keep living her dreams that she convinced her parents to let her be homeschooled from the eighth grade onward. Solange continued to tour with Destiny's Child and for a while had everything she wanted until she damaged her knee dancing on tour when she was fifteen. After losing her main mode of expression, Solange focused on writing, filling up teenage journals. Though she may not always have realized it, she had a knack for crafting intricate stories. She started writing songs at the age of nine, and in fourth grade she won a statewide competition to write a new jingle for the nonprofit organization United Way, which boosted her confidence in her writing.

In the letter written for *Teen Vogue*, Solange shared a trio of photos of herself as a teenager, each one documenting a different stage. The first image seems to be from her aforementioned Goth phase, as she poses on a staircase in black lipstick, with blond highlights running through her dark brown braids, wearing a velvet bomber jacket, rolled-up jogger pants, and a pair of Timberlands. The second image is ripe to be memed, as Solange stares directly at the camera, head tilted in defiance, dressed in an all-white off-the-shoulder outfit with a fur trim. She has the confidence of a girl ready to tell the world exactly what's on her mind. The third demonstrates the mercurial nature of teenage moods, as Solange sits, hands clasped in her lap, head tilted down, eyes toward the floor in a burgundy coat and fur gilet. She looks solemn, caught in her thoughts, away from the world. Of the three moods, my teenage years could best be summed up by the third image. I was an emo girl at heart, but I never had the confidence to openly combine the multitude of influences that I drew from. In the deepest corner of my mind, I had the wittiest clapbacks in all of Wolverhampton, but in reality, like many teenage girls, I hid myself and learned how to disappear. It is a testament to Solange's upbringing and confidence that she did not give in to the disappearing act that takes away so many teenage girls' dreams.

GOD GIVEN NAME

By the time Solange was born, the Knowles family had just a few years to prepare for the whirlwind journey Beyoncé's talent and Mathew Knowles's drive would whisk them away on. After a dance teacher noticed her singing ability at around six years old, baby Bey was catapulted into a world of talent shows and singing competitions. Given the five-year age gap, the attention Beyoncé's career demanded, and the bizarre reality that Beyoncé was a local celebrity already by her teen years, it would be understandable if the two sisters had grown apart from one another. In fact, however, their unwavering love for one another and steadfast support of each other's work has become as nourishing to witness as the music both artists create. Beyoncé describes herself as Solange's "biggest fan," while Solange claims Beyoncé did a "kickass job" of being her big sister, adding, "You were the most patient, loving, wonderful sister ever. In the 30 years that we've been together, I think we've only really, like, butted heads . . . we can count on one hand."[7]

The healthy relationship they share was helped by an early intervention from their mother, who noticed Beyoncé's rising status and how it could affect family dynamics. By the time Solange was seven, Girl's Tyme, an early incarnation of Destiny's Child, had appeared on *Star Search* (which would later be documented on Beyoncé's 2013 self-titled album) and later opened for r&b groups like SWV and Dru Hill. Given her nascent career, the pre-teen Beyoncé wasn't interested in hanging out with her little sister. In an effort to avoid conflict and resentment, Tina proactively sent the girls to therapy. As a child, Lawson felt that her mother loved her brother more than her and wanted to make sure history didn't repeat itself for her children. She dedicated days to each girl, taking time off work to be with them. Though those around her thought the counseling sessions were slightly extreme, she persevered. "My family was, like, 'You're going to make them crazy because they're too young for you to take them,' but I wanted Beyoncé to be sensitive to the fact that Solange had to deal with being a little bit in her shadow," explained Lawson. "It made her way more sensitive and protective, and they're still fiercely protective of each other."[8] We saw that protection in 2008 when Solange called out a television presenter for disrespecting her brother-in-law, plainly explaining that "that was not a very professional introduction."[9] Though the music industry and the media have consistently pitted the sisters against one another, Ms. Tina's early intervention ensured that the sisters would resist such tabloid tactics.

Their sisterly love for each other can be seen when they each joined the other on stage for their respective performances at Coachella (Solange in 2014 and Beyoncé in 2018), dancing in unison and laughing like they were performing in their mother's living room. Though Solange may have felt left out at first by Beyoncé's rigorous training for her teen girl group, the hours spent absorbing the group's regime clearly influenced a young Solange, who was already preparing for her debut release at fifteen. Her early performances were littered with the obligatory "Let me see your hands in the air," soft vocal runs, and crowd participation routines that were a staple of Destiny's Child performances.

Solange watched her sister navigate the chaos and scrutiny that comes with pop superstardom and decided she didn't want to follow the same path. Her need to avoid what she saw as the downsides of her older sister's career has shaped her journey, presenting herself as the esoteric chalk to Beyoncé's pop-savvy cheese. "God Given Name," the opening track from her 2008 second album, *Sol-Angel and the Hadley St. Dreams*, sees Solange remind the world of this fact, declaring "I'm not her and I never will be." This difference has boosted their careers and given them joint appeal, especially to Black women who worship Beyoncé's self-determined perfection, while simultaneously adoring the down-to-earth swagger Solange possesses.

FAMILY AFFAIR

Though Tina and Mathew had different approaches to parenting, they both succeeded in imbuing a sense of pride, an unwavering work ethic, and a love of Black culture in their daughters. How did these at times conflicted parents bring two superstars into the world?

By all accounts given by both sisters, their mother was a life raft in the rough waters of childhood and throughout the rocky experiences of fame. Solange tells stories of her mother that are reminiscent of many matriarchs who silently, yet diligently, hold up entire households through sheer will. When the dishes miraculously get washed, schedules are planned, and the children are given all the love and attention they need, you know an unsung mother is behind all of it. Although, like many mothers doing their best to raise their children in a patriarchal world, Lawson later felt that she focused so much on others that she never had time for herself. Looking back at her childhood, and now as a mother of one, Solange appreciated the things her mother did for her, including being a role model as a woman. "You realize watching a woman balance being a supportive mother, building a successful business from the ground up that was started in her garage, and giving back to the community will make you feel invincible and like the word 'no' is just an echo in the universe that you'll never know."[10]

To surround the girls with positive images of Black people, Tina kept an extensive collection of African American art in their home. Her collection includes work by the Houston artist Robert Pruitt, the contemporary artist Toyin Ojih Odutola, and the Texan mixed-media artist Kermit Oliver. She would gather her children around the kitchen table to conduct art history lessons, discussing the themes explored in the work she showed them. The art lessons deeply affected Solange, who, as a young teen, would visit Houston's Menil Collection and the Rothko Chapel for hours by herself.[11] Solange toured *A Seat at the Table* in museums rather than conventional music venues, created the large-scale sculpture *Metatronia (Metatron's Cube)* (2018), and wove in references to artists—such as her re-creations of British-Ghanaian painter Lynette Yiadom-Boakye's majestic depictions of Black beauty in the "Don't Touch My Hair" video—throughout her music videos.

While Tina was teaching the girls her Black-centric version of art history, Mathew's life lessons of hard work, devotion to your craft, and a business-minded outlook were also sinking in. His influence and integrity were questioned as the glamour of Destiny's Child faded and the reality of how the group became so polished at such a young age emerged (through strict training regimes and practice, which Mathew often led). What was previously seen as drive, ambition, and a need to secure a future for his family morphed into a vision of a calculated, money-hungry, pushy parent. His efforts to mold Destiny's Child into the group they became put an enormous strain on the family when he began to manage the group full-time. The family lost half their income, they had to move out of their home into a two-bedroom apartment, and Tina and Mathew briefly separated, reconciling soon after. Later revelations that Mathew fathered a child with actress Alexsandra

Wright (which prompted Tina to file for divorce in 2009) did not help his image. The affair and divorce likely caused a strain in his relationship with Beyoncé and Solange. Beyoncé announced in 2011 that she would no longer be managed by her father.

Despite Solange's love for her father, their relationship was, according to Solange, "not always very good," especially during her adolescent and young adult years.[12] The sessions for *A Seat at the Table*, where Solange brought her parents back together for the first time after their divorce, helped heal their difficult father-daughter relationship and allowed Solange to understand him. She told Billboard in 2018: "It's still very much a work in progress. But I think I have a much clearer idea of the trauma that he experienced and how it felt like it was then generationally passed on to me. Both kind of existing in the white spaces as an 'only,' and how much that can really shape and mold your experience of the world, race, and identity."[13]

Though they had their difficulties, Solange admired Mathew's business acumen, calling him a "student of Black people of power within the music industry."[14] According to Solange, Tina "taught us to be in control of our voice and our bodies and our work."[15] Dedication to Blackness and what it meant to be Black was an essential part of life in the Knowles household. All of the family members recall conversations about Black empowerment, independence, and race being a key part of family life. For Solange, those conversations started a journey toward unraveling her ancestry. "At a very young age I wanted to understand the entire lineage. I always thought there was so much power in knowing where you came from, [in order] to know where you're going."[16]

This thought process is possibly the essence of Solange and her drive. Many critics view her as an artist who rested on the Knowles name until *A Seat at the Table*. It is Solange's self-conviction, evident in the defiant actions of her youth and the boundless self-expression of her early career, which propels her forward. This conviction started in the Knowles home. Whether it was through art, history, or business, Solange was taught not only that she could do anything, but that her ancestors had already achieved wonders before her. Tracing your ancestors' footsteps to see what you find is often a necessary, if distressing, step for many in the Black diaspora. When the world tells you there's no space for you, looking back to see the multitude of examples of people who look like you not only thriving, but at the forefront of innovation, gives you the extra nugget of confidence to tell naysayers where to go.

Ultimately, Solange came from a household where her dreams were taken seriously, her emotional needs were catered to, and her talent was nurtured from an early age. It is this unconditional love that can transform the world, but too often Black women either do not receive the love they deserve or have to demand it. At a historic address at Howard University's National Black Writers Conference in 1978, the Black feminist poet and author June Jordan demanded more love in Black women's lives: "It is here, in this extreme, inviolable coincidence of my status as a Black feminist, my status as someone twice stigmatized, my status as a Black woman who is twice kin to the despised majority of all the human life that there is, . . . it is here, in this extremity, that I ask, of myself, and of anyone who would call me sister. Where is the love?"[17]

Jordan's calls for love echo those of other Black feminists who weave demands for love into their politics. In *Sisters of the Yam*, the Black feminist scholar bell hooks's seminal work on Black women and self-care, hooks surmises that love in a Black woman's life can be revolutionary. "When we as Black women experience fully the transformative power of love in our lives, we will bear witness publicly in a way that will fundamentally challenge existing social structures."[18] Hooks argues that Black women, who usually have to take care of others and grow up early and rarely receive unconditional love. When Black women do receive that love, it can be life changing, giving them the power to change the way they envision the future for Black people. For Solange, that love powered her own personal revolution—one in which she honors her family and ancestors who instilled in her a grounded sense of self, allowing her to create a new path for future generations.

POSTCOLONIAL ROOTS

Family and ancestry play a central role in *A Seat at the Table*, in Tina and Mathew's interludes, but also through

Solange's attempts to reconnect with her ancestors. Solange moved to New Iberia, Louisiana (where her mother's side of the family hail from) and stayed there for a summer on an isolated sugar plantation, where she wrote the majority of the album. Living on the grounds of the site where her people were enslaved was a "spiritually heavy experience,"[19] and she also learned the true story of why her mother's family left New Iberia. During *A Seat at the Table* recordings, Tina explained that Solange's grandfather worked in a salt mine. When a large explosion caused the mine to collapse, her grandfather and another worker were trapped underground for two days. After pleading with the mining company and getting no response, the local community dug out the men, saving their lives. The scandal proved embarrassing for the mining company, revealing the extent of their disregard for their employees' lives. In retaliation, the company hounded the workers for joining a union and eventually fired them, including Solange's grandfather. When a Molotov cocktail flew through her grandparents' window, they fled New Iberia under cover of night for Galveston, Texas, where Tina was raised.

The story of Solange's grandparents is a tale of postcolonial migration, trauma, and fear. How many families took the same road as Solange's family, and how many were stopped in their tracks before they were able to make that journey? The Great Migration of African Americans from 1916 to 1970 resulted in one of the biggest demographic shifts in the history of the United States. Around six million Black people moved away from the rural South and its segregationist policies in search of opportunity in the North and in larger cities. When they arrived in their new homes, they found a less overt kind of discrimination but one that still limited opportunities to decent housing, education, and work.

The story of migration never ends. Every day people make the sacrifice and travel to an unknown country so future generations can have a better life. We descendants of migrants often let our minds ruminate on the homes our ancestors left behind or the injustices we face in our adopted home. Rarely is much thought given to the journey, the road migrants have traveled, the cultural quirks we have picked up along the way, and the anxiety caused by displacement. It is that journey in all of its depth and raw emotion that I, like Solange, so often wanted to hear, but my family rarely offered to share it with me. I wanted to know everything: how did they feel, did they know what England would be like, or did they know if they would ever see Jamaica again? Everything I know about my family history was coerced out of my elders. At family gatherings, when everyone was merry from one too many glasses of brandy and weighed down by too many snacks, was always the best time to pounce.

Eventually through this method, I learned the full story of my dad's journey to the UK. My dad has lived most of his life in England, but he was born in the parish of Clarendon in rural Jamaica and lived there until he was eleven. In the 1950s, as a British colonial outpost, Jamaica was under the rule of the British government. Though the country was beautiful, it was mired in the legacy of slavery and colonialism, which left the country rife with inequality and little opportunity to succeed. My grandparents were a young couple with two young children they needed to provide for. They knew their best option was to move to England (eventually settling in Wolverhampton because my grandma's cousin was there after serving in the Royal Air Force during World War II), but they also knew the journey would be tough and the first few years settling in the new country even more so. Rather than raise their small children in the overcrowded shared houses many migrants had to live in while they saved for better accommodation, they left my dad and uncle in the care of their own parents in Jamaica and went to England. It was a decision many parents had to take. It was such a common occurrence that the term "barrel children" came to describe the children left behind, a reference to the barrels that were often used by the parents in other countries to send back gifts and clothing.

My dad grew up mostly unaware of his status as a barrel child and the existence of the other small island where his real parents were. My grandparents sent over whatever cash they could spare from the little they earned working in factories and doing manual labour in the Midlands, which allowed my dad to live a relatively middle-class life for Jamaica at that period. He wore the nicest shoes; lived on a five-acre farm with his extended family; and remembers collecting water from the well outside his home, climbing coconut trees, and eating fresh mangoes. The plan was going well until my grandparents had another child, and then another, and another, delaying their ability to bring my dad and uncle to live in the UK. By the time they were able to bring over my dad in 1966, he was eleven and had five other siblings in England he did not know about. Like many children, he was sent on a plane without his family and only an airline chaperone to guide him. He had no idea where he was going or why. There was some confusion when he arrived in the UK, and it eventually transpired that he was sent to the wrong airport and had to get back on a plane to Birmingham (the closest international airport to Wolverhampton). When he was reunited with my grandad, it was a shock to discover why he was really there. On the drive to Wolverhampton, my grandad stopped off at a pub and gave my dad a packet of crisps and a bottle of fizzy pop, thinking it would make him happy. He hated it. The crisps tasted vile and the artificial sweetness of the pop made him feel sick and didn't match the thirst-quenching delight of drinking fresh club soda that was popular in Jamaica. He was confused and alone and acted out by refusing to speak to my grandad for three months.

My dad eventually grew to love Wolverhampton (he regularly asks me when I'm coming back home and reminds me that he'd never live anywhere else) and has a strong connection with his family. When I discovered the full extent of my dad's journey from Jamaica to England, what he lost and gained in exchange, it explained so much about who he is as a man. He loves family more than anything, and he loves his adopted city. After all, it is the place where he found his friends, where he met my mum and had a family of his own. He found himself in the idiosyncrasies of Black British life, longing for the familiar claggy, stodgy texture of English rock cakes as much as he craves the warming, crisp bite into Jamaican fried dumplings. Pub crawls with the lads from the football club suited him just fine, but if their fun was impeded by racists, he knew how to handle himself. Bus trips to find every carnival in the country were a regular part of the summers of his youth. He still tries to convince me he knows his way around East London based solely on his overnight kips on sofas in Hackney when he and his friends traveled down to Notting Hill Carnival in the early 1980s.

While my father's journey was hard, the trauma gave him no choice but to find community and belonging in a country that made no sense to him at first. He searched for a belonging that accepted his past while creating space for reinvention and a future. It was a reinvention that so many Black British people were part of as they explored their identities and heritage. It has created some of the best moments in Black British culture, from the seductive groove of the 1970s lovers rock genre to the gritty depictions of inner-city life in grime and the many genres that have followed, such as drill and Afro bashment. Solange's grandparents also had to reinvent their lives, in Texas. For our families, there is not just trauma but also the lives they made for themselves and their families within pockets of otherwise oppressive societies. Much like Solange, I want to document my family's journey to acknowledge the life we created for ourselves and to fight against those who never wanted us here, despite the fact that they came to us first.

BACK IN THE THIRD WARD

Though the Knowles family moved out years ago, their old home in the Third Ward is now marked on Google Maps. In images posted by fans posing outside, it's obvious that the three-bedroom, three-bathroom home was a symbol of the family's wealth and achievements. A neatly landscaped garden sits in front of the southern-style stately home with towering white columns. Its opulence and class suggest it was a secure and stable neighborhood for Solange and Beyoncé to grow up in.

As with many neighborhoods, Third Ward contained opposing truths that happily coexisted. College students lived a stone's throw away from the intersection of Dowling and McGowen (in 2018, it was named one of the most dangerous areas in the United States).[20] The diverse community that resided in Third Ward was evident to Solange even as a child. She was exposed to different sides of life and believed that each was equal and a potential future for her. Whether it was the pastor's wife hurrying down the road, the overworked lawyer, the stripper, or the schoolteacher, they were all examples of strong Black women who were making the most of their lives.

It was a neighborhood that, to Solange's eye, was akin to a revived Black Wall Street, with its own Black-owned banks, schools, and grocery stores.[21] Third Ward's Black community set up their own independent businesses, including salons, barbers, funeral homes, and theaters, in the post–Civil War era. In this diverse and proud Black community, Solange saw people who refused to be defeated by discrimination and lack of opportunity; who saw independence and economic freedom—the American dream—as a possibility despite systemic racism. Third Ward's influence on Solange is most clearly seen on 2019's free-form, Afrofuturist exploration *When I Get Home*, which is laden with references to her hometown.

Third Ward has a rich tradition of producing creatives and has been home to DJ Screw, known for the chopped-and-screwed DJ technique; the influential 1990s hip-hop act Geto Boys, and the famous siblings: choreographer Debbie Allen and *Cosby Show* actress Phylicia Rashad. As such, it is an area that values the tradition of southern story-telling. "I feel like, in the South in general, but specifically in our world growing up, people were expressive and vivid storytellers," Solange said to her sister in *Interview* magazine in 2017. "In the hair salon or in the line at the grocery store; there was never a dull moment."[22]

Oral storytelling in the Black community is influenced by rhythmic patterns of speech and African American

Vernacular English (AAVE). These ways of communicating have given African Americans a sense of connection and a unique dialect that can transcend a specific region. Key phrasing or the removal of vowels in certain words can heighten a crucial moment in a story, lifting it from chuckle-inducing to room-commanding greatness in an instant. Solange uses AAVE to speak directly to the Black audience and tell a story they will know all too well. Lines such as "When a nigga tryna board a plane / and they ask you what's your name again," from 2016's "F.U.B.U.," show Solange's pride in a dialect that has been incorrectly criticized as improper English. The expectation of the song and much of Solange's catalog is that *you* must learn to understand *us*.

Through Solange's slow southern drawl, which she attributes to being a "Houston girl," the voices of her elders live and breathe in her music.[23] Her speech pattern almost surfaces in her vocal style, which, broadly, remains calm and present. Solange's ability to reflect her community and its storytelling style in her work is a skill I hope to possess. I remember being waist-high to my aunts and uncles, looking up at them as they sat around my grandparents' living room. The TV blared on full volume, but it was still drowned out by their conversation. I wanted to join in, to understand what they were saying, to laugh as loudly and as fully as they did, gesticulating with their whole bodies, debating everything from politics to that year's Christmas episode of a TV soap. It is in those moments, in our salons, our stores, our grandmother's living rooms, that we see our elders as free as they can possibly be—not stifled by overbearing bosses, uncaring landlords, or the weight of the world. They are free to live in the depths of Black joy, taking care to savor every moment. As an artist, no matter what I'm creating, I hope to achieve a sensation of true happiness like those moments gave me; that will always be my end goal.

— 3 —

THE MAKING OF A SOLO STAR

It is almost an industry standard to deploy a mini version of a successful artist to cash in on their likeness and reach the coveted preteen audience. Janet Jackson followed Michael, Noah Cyrus became a child star like her sister Miley, and Solange was ready to step into the spotlight created by Destiny's Child. Though one may assume the pressure to join her sister on stage came from her parents or label bosses, Solange made the choice herself. Her parents protested at first, concerned that Solange was too young, but they eventually gave in, and Solange was set to be the next bright young thing from Knowles HQ.

She started working on her debut at fourteen after signing with Columbia Records. The direction for the album came from a multitude of avenues, some of which were worlds apart. While on holiday in Jamaica with her family, Solange fell in love with Rastafari culture, a religious and political Afrocentric movement, which began in Jamaica in the 1930s following the coronation of Haile Selassie as emperor of Ethiopia. The Rastafari movement believes Selassie is the second coming of Christ and emphasizes living naturally, adhering to vegan Ital diets, and wearing their hair in dreadlocks. Solange's obsession continued once she came home, driving her to grow her hair down past her waist and to weave reggae beats into her album demos, to the unease of her label. Reflecting on that time, Solange told an audience at Yale University in 2017: "When I came out with my first album when I was 15, *Solo Star*, I had dabbled with some downbeat electronic music, I had Brothers Johnson playing guitar on my music. I really wanted to make this Sade-esque record at 15 [audience laughs] and the label did what y'all did."[1]

A teenager demanding to make a reggae-tinged lovers rock album would be enough to make any label executive nervous. Solange's vision couldn't have been further from their expectations or from the output of her contemporaries. Decked out in low-slung hip-hugging jeans, crop tops, and pierced belly buttons, the era's top stars were all-American beauties who made cookie-cutter, bubblegum pop that alluded to a fully grown sexuality. Compared to teen pop icon Britney Spears's regimented, hook-heavy gloss, the multigenre concoction Solange originally conceived looked almost otherworldly to bottom-line-focused label executives. Despite the rejection of her initial plans, the *Solo Star* artwork and music videos are littered with the Rastafari imagery. On the album cover, Solange wears a bohemian knit cap over her shoulder-length red and brown braids. The same themes appear in the video for her debut single, "Feelin' You (Part II)," as Solange dances at a cookout in front of the symbolic red, gold, and green colors of the Rastafari flag (based on the original Ethiopian flag). For many Rastas, the colors carry meaning; red represents the blood of dead activists; gold represents the sun, religious freedom, and wealth of Africa; and green symbolizes the fertile vegetation of the earth. It was a small nod to her original theme and an early sign of the tenacity of her artistic vision, as well as her commitment to a pro-Black aesthetic.

In the run-up to the album release, Mathew Knowles pulled every trick in the book to entice the world to pay attention to Solange, whom he managed under his enterprise Music World Entertainment. Solange sang lead vocals—backed by Destiny's Child—on the theme tune to the Disney Channel's all-Black cartoon *The Proud Family* and appeared as the teen rapper Lil' Bow Wow's date in his music video "Puppy Love." With her name recognition growing by the week, Solange was ready to enter the teen pop market. *Solo Star* was released on December 26, 2002. The record was packed with some of the biggest names in the charts at the time, with everyone from production duo the Neptunes—who had already made hit songs with artists like Jay-Z and Britney Spears—to r&b producer Timbaland, known for his work with Aaliyah and Missy Elliott, lending a hand. Even big sister Beyoncé was there behind the scenes working on the production and lyrics and helping to pick a standout single, "Feelin' You."

The album was not a hit, reaching only no. 23 in the Billboard Top R&B/Hip-Hop charts. Critics gave little leeway to the teen star and openly resented the nepotism at play, given the family's connections. Writing for *Slant* magazine, the journalist Sal Cinquemani wrote: "Solange takes the notion 'It's all about who you know' to ridiculous new heights with the lackluster *Solo Star*."[2] Though critics balked at the sheer number of A-list producers on her album, one figure in her life caught their attention: Beyoncé. It was the beginning of the media's obsession with comparing the sisters. To some, they seemed too alike. To others, Solange didn't live up to Beyoncé's diva status. For the critic J. Victoria Sanders, Solange was making choices only to be seen as different from her sister, a theory that followed Solange for years. In a review for *Pop Matters*, Sanders said: "If you love the harmonies and attitude of Destiny's Child and you were looking for Beyoncé's mini-me, this is the wrong album for you. Solange's angle is precisely that: that she's doing her own thing, independent of the Knowles family tradition for flamboyance on and off-stage."[3]

Solo Star is a product of its time, but it does not give listeners an understanding of just how infectiously fun this era in pop was. The production flattens out Solange's already wispy vocals, which were not developed enough at the time to reach the range she aimed for. Much of the album feels like a showcase for the producer rather than the artist, as Solange's voice fades into the background of a barrage of lovelorn ballads and made-for-the-club hits. Even the label's pragmatic decision to confine her to the urban market backfired. The album still contains hints of Solange's eclectic style, which, without context or structure, renders the record bloated and confusing. Despite its flaws, the album was an early indicator of Solange's greatest strengths. She wrote the lyrics for the majority of the songs and produced several tracks, a role she would continue as her career progressed. The Neptunes, however, produced and penned one of the few standout moments on the debut, "Crush." The duo paired high-pitched '80s-inspired synths with trigger-happy drum beats and a cute breathy sample of a sigh of relief. It is one of the few tracks on which Solange's voice is centered and matches the mood of the song. Upbeat and sassy, "Crush" plays perfectly on her youth, describing a teenage infatuation other girls could relate to. Lead single "Feelin' You" is more in line with a modern-day version of Solange. The warped pan pipes, which loop over and over, and chopped-up beat are an ode to Houston's DJ Screw.

The move from writing songs in her bedroom as a mode of self-expression to having outsiders comment on her ideas was difficult for the teenager to handle. She told MTV in 2002: "So from that point on, I was like, 'I've gotta learn how to arrange and produce my own music, 'cause this is too hard for me.'"[4] Her ability to adapt and try again is rare in a young artist. This desire to be part of every step of creating a song set the stage for the auteur Solange we know today. Speaking in 2009, Solange pointed to her age and inexperience as contributing factors to the album's sound: "I knew what kind of artist I wanted to be, but I didn't know how to carry it out. And I wasn't brave enough to carry it out because I was more concerned with pleasing my label."[5] The admission that she had little power to change the minds of the rich white men who categorized her in line with their understanding of what Black girls could create was not given with a sense of despair. Rather, it is a statement of fact.

In the early 2000s, the big money resided in the pop-lite r&b stars who made songs about the highs and lows of relationships. One of the biggest r&b acts of 2002 was the platinum-selling artist Ashanti, who could transform seamlessly from hip-hop's favorite ride-or-die girl to purveyor of deceptively sweet pop classics, all in her delicate, breathy vocals. Singer Amerie, known for her 2004 hit "One Thing," also fit neatly into the pop r&b mold. Both women made their names using the formula handed to every Black woman in r&b: use high production values and upbeat melodies to produce songs about heartbreak or new love that could also double as a summertime party anthem. Although the formula produced many great songs and made these women famous, it centered on masculinity, how the women related to men and, generally, relied on male producers or rappers to break a new female artist into the industry. The rapper Ja Rule frequently collaborated with Ashanti after the two were paired together by their label, Murder Inc. Records.

The formula rarely allowed for experimentation or for its female artists to be more than just pretty faces with angelic voices. Solange, in her youthful ambition, was reaching toward an art-pop, experimental sound similar to the iconic Icelandic producer and singer-songwriter Björk, who, despite gaining mainstream success, has managed to distance herself from the pop world with her avant-garde eccentricities. Björk was born in Reykjavík, the daughter of a feminist activist mother and a union leader electrician father. From the age of five, she attended a children's music school, where she studied classical music theory and released an album at eleven years old. She spent her teen years in a number of punk and anarchist bands, surrounded by the scene's strident DIY ethos and bohemian lifestyle. Her success with the Icelandic alt-pop band the Sugarcubes and her early solo records were driven by her punk principles and a desire for new musical forms of expression. She has fused elements of jazz, experimental, house, IDM (intelligent dance music), pop, techno, classical, and trip-hop in her sound over the years. What holds these disparate elements together is Björk herself.

Björk's vision for each album expanded beyond the music to include photography, videos, fashion, and even an app for the 2011 album *Biophilia*. To achieve this world-building concept, she worked closely with other artists, musicians, and producers, aligning each collaboration to the specificity of each song and the story she needed to tell. Her 1999 video for "All Is Full of Love," directed by Chris Cunningham, which depicts a passionate love scene between two robots, was inspired by Björk's description of the song as being where love and lust meet, using two ivory statues as a visual example for Cunningham. She also coproduced and coarranged the majority of her back catalog, though the praise was often directed solely at her collaborators, an issue that aggravated her over the years. Despite outsiders' confusion over who was in charge, it is safe to say that Björk is and was the director of all her creative explorations. Solange exhibits the same professional curiosity, the same gift for expanding her work beyond the boundaries of music, and the same DIY attitude to every aspect of her musical and visual output in her own avant-garde creations.

A modern example of Solange's teenage vision could be seen in the teen pop star Billie Eilish, who merges the worlds of emo, whispered ASMR-like vocals, and pop with seemingly little restriction from her label. Eilish was born in Los Angeles in 2001 to a family of actors and musicians. Her mother homeschooled Eilish and her older brother, Finneas, and taught them the basics of songwriting. Eilish came to prominence with the viral hit "Ocean Eyes," a cover of a song Finneas wrote for his own band, released when she was fourteen. The dream pop simplicity of "Ocean Eyes" was a world away from the melee of genres that converged on her 2019 debut album, *When We All Fall to Sleep, Where Do We Go?* With Finneas on production again, they blended synth pop with drowsy West Coast SoundCloud rap, percussive EDM beats with industrial noise. The album was a commercial and critical success, landing at number one on the Billboard 200 chart, helping Eilish to win five Grammys and two American Music Awards. At eighteen, she is also the youngest person to perform a title song for a James Bond film, *No Time to Die* (released November 2020) following in the footsteps of British stars Adele and Sam Smith.

Eilish had good timing, emerging in an industry that has come to terms with the genreless void many listeners occupy thanks to streaming. Working with her brother (recording the album in their bedrooms), Eilish could experiment with a collaborator she trusted, in a space where she felt comfortable. The bedroom pop connected with millions of teenage fans who saw themselves in Eilish's teen Goth outlook. Even before her album release, Eilish commanded a strong fan base who found her on the music-sharing platform SoundCloud or through word of mouth. Though Eilish is signed to a major record label (Darkroom, an imprint of Interscope Records), the industry is well aware of the connection pop stars need to have with their fan base on social media. In an era when lifestyle influencers and YouTube vloggers have as much effect on youth culture as any artist, it helps if young pop stars appear approachable and relatable. Too much interference from a label would interrupt this winning formula Eilish uses. This allowed Eilish to relax into herself and develop the style people know her for.

As a young white woman, Eilish's use of Black culture has helped her stand out—and led her into trouble. Some have accused her of cultural appropriation, as her fashion style is highly influenced by late '90s hip-hop culture, and she often uses AAVE in her speech. Also, in an interview in the March 2020 issue of *Vogue* magazine, Eilish was accused of making dismissive statements about hip-hop, a genre she drew from heavily, when talking about authenticity and character-driven writing. The offhand comment struck a nerve and echoed similar statements made by white artists, like pop star Miley Cyrus, who use the genre as a way to gain notoriety but still feel they have the authority to critique it. For an artist who is presented as reinventing pop, making music for a generation that knows hip-hop as a mainstream genre, it is understandable that many found Eilish's privilege to be showing here. In 2002, a year after Eilish was born, the prospect of Solange using hip-hop to *stand out* was ridiculous; mainstream audiences *assumed* a Black teenager would already be into hip-hop culture.

Oddly, the artist I feel most reflects Solange's youthful curiosity is the English singer-songwriter and national treasure Kate Bush—someone Solange has referred to as an icon. Bush was also a child prodigy and began writing songs at eleven years old. She released the quirky quasi-Gothic hit "Wuthering Heights" at age nineteen as the lead single from her debut album *The Kick Inside* in 1978. Her label was unhappy with the single, finding it too unusual. They pushed her to first release the more commercially viable prog rock song "James and the Cold Gun," but Bush stood her ground. She won and was proved right instantly. "Wuthering Heights" sold over a million copies in the UK, and Bush became the first woman in the UK to reach the number-one spot on the charts with a self-penned song.

Though it is impossible to directly compare the two artists, who each have their own singular vision and are from different generations, it is hard not to feel a sense of loss for Solange. She could have realized her voice as an artist much earlier if she had the confidence of an English middle-class white girl like Bush, who once reportedly described herself as "the shyest megalomaniac you're ever likely to meet."[6] Both were talented young women determined to see their unconventional ideas put in place. Though the music industry dismissed them both at first, Bush's white middle-class privilege gave her confidence and helped the white male executives give in to her demands, as they were likely from a similar background and could relate to her. Solange's teenage Black girl weirdo self did not appeal to the label executives Bush won over, and she therefore struggled to put across her views. It is hard to say what could or should have happened with *Solo Star*, but like Bush, Solange remained focused on her goal. Though she took herself out of the limelight for a few years, she continued to work on her craft and hone her vision. In the years to come, she would continue to make her own legacy, fulfilling her childhood dreams, just as Bush did.

IN TRANSITION

In the aftermath of *Solo Star*, Solange formed a jazz band with her friends (by her own word, they weren't very good), and tried to get back to everyday life, but as she reached her seventeenth birthday, her world turned on its head. In 2004, her best friend Marsai Song was killed by a stray bullet in a drive-by shooting. Within a year of this tragic incident, Solange found herself pregnant. The father was her childhood sweetheart, Daniel Smith. The pair met at a high school party when Solange was thirteen and, after finding out they were pregnant, wed when Solange was seventeen and Smith was nineteen.

Her pregnancy and marriage came as a shock to the rest of the world, but Solange was determined. She prepared a detailed birthing plan. Sade's "By Your Side" set the mood for the day, and she asked for quiet in the room so she could remain "focused" on bringing her child into the world.[7] She gave birth to Daniel Julez J. Smith Jr. on October 18, 2004, describing the birth as "the first time I felt unconditional love in such a strong way."[8]

Solange and her young family moved to Moscow, Idaho, where Daniel played football at the University of Idaho. The move from the bustling, multicultural city of Houston to a small town, which, according to the last census in 2010 has a population of 23,800 and is 90.1 percent white, was a difficult adjustment for the couple.[9] Speaking to the *Spokesman Review* in 2005 about his football career and the move, Smith said: "It's slow, but it gives us a lot of good family time. It's 3 million (people) versus 20,000, but we're here for a purpose and we're trying to get it accomplished."[10] Solange became a doting football wife and mother, who brought her son to games and cheered loudly from the side of the field.

Slowly, though, living in a small town away from everyone she knew became all-consuming. Speaking to *Elle* in 2017, she said: "It was one of the most bittersweet moments of my life because I was so in love with Julez, and having spent a lot of time on the road, I yearned to be in one place, to have the opportunity to really ground myself with him. But it was isolating and lonely, and so cold and dark. And it was just Julez and me most of the time. It was hard to imagine being able to progress in my career in any way."[11] Solange felt trapped in the new life and sought a way out through acting and songwriting. She had already appeared in the comedy *Johnson Family Vacation* in 2004, and in 2006 she took on the starring role of cheerleading captain Camille in the teen film *Bring It On: All or Nothing*. Despite her new identity as a rural housewife, Solange continued to write for other musicians. She had previously written and produced "The Movement" from Destiny's Child member Michelle Williams's 2004 solo album, *Do You Know*. She also contributed her songwriting skills to the confessional breakup bop "Love" on Kelly Rowland's 2007 album, *Ms. Kelly*, and "Bad Habit" from Destiny Child's final album, *Destiny Fulfilled* (2004).

To understand Solange's development as a songwriter

during this period one only has to look at her work with her sister. On Beyoncé's 2006 high-energy, funky yet frank sophomore release, *B'Day*, Solange contributed to the dancefloor hit, "Get Me Bodied." Beyoncé was inspired by her relationships with Solange, Kelly, and Michelle to create the girls' night out classic. Solange joined the writing team and helped shape the song along with her cousin Angela Beyincé, songwriter Makeba Riddick, songwriter and producer Sean Garrett, and hip-hop producer Swizz Beatz. "Get Me Bodied" is built on a steady roll of furious handclaps and a hearty chorus of shouted "heys" and "jumps" that amplify the energy of the track. The song embodies the inclusivity of a playground chant or traditional African American work song in which call-and-response lyrics and instructive descriptions give everyone a chance to participate. It is also an early example of Beyoncé creating for her community, including directions to dance by patting your weave or doing the Naomi Campbell walk just like the famous Black British supermodel.

Like the cool little sister she is, Solange has continued to inspire the monumental popstar, leading Beyoncé onto unconventional paths she would otherwise never wander down. The '70s Funkadelic-inspired "Why Don't You Love Me," released in 2010, was written by Solange in 2008 after working with the Houston-based producers Bama Boyz on her sophomore album, *Sol-Angel and the Hadley St. Dreams*. When Solange asked the production team to send over some demos for her to work on for her sister, the Bama Boyz weren't sure the instrumentation would suit Beyoncé, but they sent it over anyway. Solange loved the track, and conceived the anthem for every downtrodden partner looking for the perfect soundtrack to accompany packing their bags, setting their other half's best clothes on fire on the front lawn, and leaving their sorry cheating ass.

Solange's contributions to her sister's back catalog extend far beyond writing credits. As the younger sibling, removed from the stifling Destiny's Child training regime, Solange enjoyed a level of freedom and teenage rebellion Beyoncé was unable to partake in. As a result, Beyoncé lived vicariously through her sister, learning how to take on the outspoken traits and self-assured persona Solange presents. In one of her first openly political songs, "***Flawless" from 2013's self-titled *Beyoncé* (a critically acclaimed album that broke new ground for her as an artist), Beyoncé declares who was behind her newfound outlook on life, exclaiming, "My sister told me I should speak my mind." Solange's presence can also be found on Beyoncé's seminal 2016 visual album, *Lemonade*, for which the production credits read like the contacts list of Solange's phone. The British indie artist James Blake, who has released music on Solange's Saint Records label, features, along with the producer MeLo-X, who was introduced to Beyoncé at Solange's New Year's Eve party. The visual album saw Beyoncé play the scorned wife of a cheating husband, taking the audience on a journey from anger to acceptance and forgiveness. *Lemonade* is a document of female endurance, with themes of intergenerational healing, diasporic African culture, and anti–police brutality. *A Seat at the Table* and *Lemonade* being released in the same year and sharing similar themes led to many comparisons. Some viewed the sisters' albums as two halves of one truth. While it is important to view each album on its own, both capturing differing aspects of the Black female experience, it is clear that Solange was part of the *Lemonade* mood board. Her influence allowed Beyoncé to find her voice and in turn inspire so many other Black women to be heard also. It is not too grandiose to make the claim that without Solange as a guide, the Beyoncé as we know her now and *Lemonade* would not exist.

Back in 2005, Solange was still Beyoncé's guide from afar, as she remained in Moscow, Idaho. The period was so disorienting that even Solange herself tweeted in 2017, "I often forget I lived in Idaho."[12] Cut off from her family, she missed her mother the most and comforted herself by listening to the '60s girl groups Tina loved and was briefly a part of (while in high school, Tina was in a vocal harmony group called the Veltones). This aural comfort blanket seeped into her consciousness, providing the backbone for her next reinvention.

HEARTBREAK AND RETRO SOUL

By the time Solange made her second album, the music industry had moved on from the squeaky clean pop that dominated the charts in 2002. The US charts in 2008 were packed with ballad-weary singers like Keyshia Cole and Alicia Keys, while unabashedly, flamboyant dance floor fillers like Usher's "Love in This Club" became the high point of many a night out. Solange, too, had moved on. She divorced her husband in 2007 and moved to Los Angeles with her son. By the time she returned to Houston and started working on her second album, around 2007, she was a world-weary, divorced single mom who had an abundance of observations on heartbreak and loss to inject into her music.

Sol-Angel and the Hadley St. Dreams was released on August 26, 2008, and debuted at number nine on the Billboard 200 chart. The album is a kaleidoscopic blast of 1960s soul and '70s blues with slivers of European trance and hypnotizing ambient pop in the mix. The choice to focus on Motown, an era responsible for some of the most succinct depictions of heartbreak ever recorded, was particularly apt, given that she was coming to terms with her recent divorce. While *A Seat at the Table* is thought to be her family tribute album, the Knowles's influence is all over *Sol-Angel*. Tina's love for sequins and booming harmonies, made popular by acts from the '60s like Detroit's Martha and the Vandellas and original bad girls the Ronettes, pours out of the record. On the lead single "I Decided," Solange very literally weaves her inspiration into the fabric of the song; sampling handclaps from the Supremes and bringing Lamont Dozier (one-third of the Motown-era hit-making production team Holland-Dozier-Holland) into writing sessions for the album. Solange's glamorous ode to Tina was not the only Knowles reference on the project, as the album title is a nod to her father and refers to a plot of land where he built his business. The album title and musical references demonstrate that Solange is a continuation of the dreams and achievements of her parents. Solange is throwing on the sequined gowns and matching bejeweled earrings her mother would have adorned herself with in her own girl group. She is creating her own future in the studio her father built from the ground up.

Alongside her retro soul influences, Solange was also keen to showcase her eclectic tastes. She collaborated with several producers, including Mark Ronson (known for his 2007 album *Version* and his work with UK soul singer Amy Winehouse), Gnarls Barkley's CeeLo Green, Jack Splash (who worked with r&b acts like Alicia Keys and John Legend), and the Danish production team Soulshock and Karlin. The duo previously worked with r&b legends like Toni Braxton and Destiny's Child, which is how Solange was first introduced to them. I spoke by email to Carsten Schack, one-half of the production duo, who remembers Solange connecting with them over their European dance background. "Growing up in Europe, music was less categorised and things got mixed up together without thinking so much what genre it was," says Schack. "It was clear for us that Solange wanted to do something different and we loved it."[13]

They got to work developing demos she brought to them

and writing songs with her from scratch. They produced "Sandcastle Disco," a peppy summer dance hit that plays on the chaotic nature of emotional fragility, and the experimental psychedelic soul collaboration with the neo-soul singer Bilal, "Cosmic Journey." The latter sees Solange push herself far beyond her usual boundaries to create a six-minute hazy, electro-indie number that veers dramatically from smooth art-pop gloss into an electrifyingly infectious trance coda. Schack recalls the team and Solange spending hours poring over an array of references, from Björk to dance music veterans the Chemical Brothers, British electronic duo Frou Frou, and Scottish ambient group Boards of Canada. Drawing on the influences from her childhood touring Europe with Destiny's Child, Solange strove to reach the level of creative expression she always desired. As Schack remembers, "She kept pushing us to go as left as we can—and Karlin and I can definitely go left."[14] Unfortunately, it is the prematurely forced nature of her expression and her desire to be among her heroes that render the song lacking and its influences showcased far too garishly.

As well as drawing from a smorgasbord of musical influences, Solange found lyrical inspiration from her own life. She delved into the perils of one-night stands ("T.O.N.Y."), relived the worst of relationship breakdowns ("Would've Been the One"), and came out of the shadow of her older sibling ("God Given Name"). Her honesty and expansive musical exploration made a far better impression on the press than her debut and garnered generally positive reviews. In 2008, the journalist Priya Elan saw Solange's underdog status as the drive that fueled her creativity. In a review for the UK newspaper the *Times*, Elan wrote: "*Sol-Angel* . . . is no Winehouse-come-lately pastiche, however. With the help of such luminaries as Gnarls Barkley's Cee-Lo, she has created a modern classic."[15] I spoke to Elan to hear his reflections on the album a decade later, and he still feels as positively about *Sol-Angel* . . . as he did in 2008. "What I liked about it was from "T.O.N.Y." onwards you had a sense of this is a woman in her twenties living her life and going through stuff," says Elan. "You felt connected to Solange as an artist. I don't think before, one knew who Solange really was, so this was an introduction to her as a person."[16]

"T.O.N.Y." also caught the ear of another music journalist at the time, Keith Murphy, who was a senior editor for *Vibe* magazine in 2008. Impressed by Solange's style, Murphy asked his editor in chief, Danyel Smith, if he could profile her for the magazine. The single spoke to Murphy, who was enthused by Solange's esoteric nature. "It was cheeky, it was throwback, it was smart," Murphy told me. "It was kind of like if Amy Winehouse grew up in Texas and happened to be the baby sister of one of the biggest r&b pop stars in the business."[17] Murphy and Elan were not alone in their leap to connect Solange with the English pop icon Amy Winehouse, who tragically died of alcohol poisoning in 2011. Winehouse's name appeared prominently in countless *Sol-Angel* . . . album reviews. Although the two artists are singular in their own way, the most obvious connection between the two women lies with Winehouse's collaborator, the producer Mark Ronson, whose sole contribution to *Sol-Angel* . . . was production on "6 O'Clock Blues." The song features Winehouse's backing band the Dap Kings, who were sampled along with the soul legend and the Dap Kings' original frontwoman Sharon Jones. For some reviewers, *Sol-Angel* . . . followed Winehouse's lauded 2006 release *Back to Black* and therefore seemed insignificant next to the burgeoning retro soul movement taking place in the UK, where stars like Duffy, Adele, and Winehouse played on the UK's history of blue-eyed soul. The combination of bad timing on her release cycle and Winehouse's dominance in the public eye (partly due to her tabloid notoriety) chained *Sol-Angel* . . . in some journalists' minds to the retro soul movement of the 2000s.

During the album release cycle, Solange spoke often about how desperately she needed to return to music. Making the album brought her out of her self-imposed isolation in Idaho to vent about her relationship breakdown. She described the journey of creation as being like "traveling through the past, present and future of my emotions."[18] The album did represent a new path for Solange as an artist and a woman at a turning point in her life. Lyrically, we see the development of Solange as a candid writer, able to filter through the dramatic, door-slamming rows that we often remember as defining a failed relationship to focus on her own state of mind. On the bonus track "White Picket Dreams," Solange analyzes her failed marriage and need for stability and domestic bliss:

> It's possible I dream such a thing that's so far away
> And the flame that you bring is warming up
> It's possible we all want a dream that's so far away
> And my white picket dreams are home enough

She muses that her dreams of the perfect marriage were just that—dreams that were made reality only for a short time. Dreams do not have to die. They can remain alive, leaving her open to the prospect of living within the boundaries of that white picket fence again. Dreams can also be "home enough," far more enticing in your head than the real thing. Solange's inner life is also evident on the laidback, summertime soul of the opener "God Given Name," as grand a pop music mission statement as any out there, and "This Bird" (which samples Boards of Canada's "Slow This Bird Down"), a self-soothing, blissed-out track about pushing ahead in spite of any negativity in the way.

Her dedication to creating a record that captures the heart of '60s and '70s soul is commendable but wears thin at various moments. Though songs like "Dancing in the Dark" and "6 O'Clock Blues" so precisely incorporate the flawless harmonies, peppy brass sections, and fourth-wall-breaking addresses to the listener heard on any Tamla Records B-side, the choice to only recreate leaves little that is new for the listener to take away. Rather, the lesser moments on the album feel like Solange has merely rewritten her own lyrics over older popular songs. It makes for a great first listen, but no matter how many times I play them, the songs refuse to find a place in my head.

The genre-traversing artist that Solange became is clearly awakening on this album, but she feels like a chef who has all the right ingredients in front of her but picks an imperfect recipe to execute her dish. Perhaps excited to have more creative freedom than she had previously held, Solange packed everything into the record without considering whether she needed to. In a review of the album, the *Pitchfork* contributor Tim Finney locked in on what seemed to be Solange's main hindrance at this point: "It's not a case of Solange performing best when she jettisons her ambition, but rather her need to find a way to let her avant inclinations work with rather than against her pop instincts, and maybe the best way for that to happen is to let the former emerge organically through the latter."[19]

FUCK THE INDUSTRY

Solange was understandably frustrated by critics' need to place her in the retro soul movement. Speaking to Keith Murphy in 2008, Solange said: "I didn't make an album that sounds like Amy or even Duffy because they didn't create '60s soul music. I made a record that sounds like The Marvelettes or The Supremes."[20] Solange had a clear vision of how she saw herself and made it known to Murphy that she wasn't about to be put in a box. "She was naming all of these indie rock acts that she liked at the time, Grizzly Bear, a few other acts," recalls Murphy. "And I kind of knew what she was doing; she was dropping it in there like, 'Don't peg me as the usual Black girl just trying to be weird, trying to be different in this space, because I don't wanna be known as r&b. You're going to respect the fact that my taste colors what I'm doing right now. There's a reason why I am doing the music that I'm doing now.' And it's less about trying to be the new r&b chick, and more just trying to be Solange."[21]

Though Geffen Records publicly declared their support for Solange's esoteric project and saw generous album sales, Solange and the label parted ways. She has since reflected that she felt uncomfortable at the time with her label, which wanted to confine her to what she described as the "grown and sexy" category, a label that Solange believed was carelessly pinned on many Black women in r&b and pop.[22] Solange refers to a category of Black women who are restrained by the wants of major labels, allowed to sing about love and relationships, be soulful, but still have to look cute and make sure they bring out a dance hit. Solange at the time felt uncomfortable in that role. Performing at an Atlanta event with the Black British singer and rapper Estelle, Solange exclaimed to the crowd: "Radios and programmers don't know what to do with us, but you guys do."[23] She knew the audience wanted something different, but the industry had not yet caught up. She leaked the song, "Fuck the Industry," intended for a mixtape she never released, in which she pleaded to her audience not to tear her personality away from her to fit into the restrictive mold society expects Black women to fill. She protests:

> I'll never be picture perfect Beyoncé
> Fly like J-Lo or singing Baby like 'Shanti
> . . .
> And I got soul in my soul but not quite like Mary
> Ain't nothing really r&b about me

Though she was well versed in the history and nuances of r&b, once telling an interviewer, "I live, eat and breathe r&b music," Solange began to feel pigeonholed.[24] Many other Black artists have espoused similar sentiments. Speaking to *The Quietus* in 2011, the reclusive singer-songwriter Frank Ocean said: "If you're a singer and you're Black, you're an r&b artist. Period."[25] In a *Pitchfork* article about Black musicians who felt restricted by expectations to be r&b, the electronic folk artist (also Solange's friend and collaborator) Moses Sumney spoke about his frustrations with the industry. "When we put Black artists in these boxes, we strip their ability to morph—which is something white artists don't have to deal with."[26] As a Black woman who spent most of her childhood in majority Black spaces and was truly connected to her history, Solange was saddened to realize that she had to navigate rules around what was or wasn't Black. Feeling that she couldn't be truly inventive in what she saw as a restrictive space for Black women in mainstream r&b, Solange made the choice to work with independent labels, which, to her mind, allowed artists to experiment and grow creatively. This led to a period during which she became every indie blogger's favorite soul singer—an experience that would quickly sour, but it was a necessary catalyst that would inspire her most-lauded work.

— 4 —

BITE THE HAND, IT NEVER FED YOU

Post *Sol-Angel and the Hadley St. Dreams*, Solange was left without a label or a direction. Her album was a composite of the music she loved, but still she felt she had hit a glass ceiling in her attempt to communicate her style to a wider audience. Though she parted ways with her label, *Sol-Angel's* . . . multigenre aesthetic did lead her to a die-hard group of fans who would follow her no matter what. During an interview with *Vibe* magazine in 2010, she commented: "Being able to tour and actually see and touch the people who are trying to really hear and feel your music is how you actually see what your fanbase is made of. These folks were not just people who wanted a radio song or wanted a particular record just for the catchiness of it. I had the people who were true music lovers; those kinds of fans will grow with me. If I want to do something more adventurous they won't abandon me."[1] With a sense of acceptance from a fan base she loved, she ventured further and further beyond the r&b scene on a journey that would take her to the scuffed-Converse-wearing, obscure '80s new wave band–T-shirt-owning, ironically cool world of the hipsters who ruled Brooklyn indie rock.

"Indie rock" is a pretty loose term. First coined in reference to independent labels, the term "indie rock" morphed to describe the music made by bands on those labels. As the music industry changed in the early 2000s (due to falling album sales and an uneasy transition to digital) and indie bands grew in popularity, the term was used to describe any alternative-sounding guitar band, whether they were signed to a major or an independent label. Throughout this book, I use the term "indie rock" or "indie" in reference to guitar rock–centric or experimental electronic bands who may have, at some point in their career, been associated with independent labels and the community around them. The indie rock and punk scenes I experienced in the 2000s were predominantly white, in terms of the people who took up space and were celebrated in the scene. It does not mean there were no people of color there, but I highlight the fact that many people of color were often pushed to the sidelines and were rarely on stage. This also does not mean punk or indie rock are genres that are "white" in any way. My own search for belonging through punk led me to the roots of rock 'n' roll and showed me that it was the flamboyant, guttural guitar riffs of the gospel performer Sister Rosetta Tharpe that inspired the hip-swaying allure of Elvis and the pioneering brash guitar licks of Chuck Berry, and laid the seeds for the greatest innovations in guitar-based music. When I connect my fingers with my guitar fretboard and feel the notes surge up my arm and into my chest, I know I'm following in the footsteps of so many of my ancestors who have gone before me.

The whiteness of indie rock matters because the participants' poor understanding of race and unexamined privilege had a lasting effect on Solange, and it all started back in August 2009 at a free Grizzly Bear show in Williamsburg, New York. At the gig, onlookers tried to focus on the cerebral indie act but couldn't keep their eyes on the stage. As they swayed to the band's haunting rhythms, to the side of the stage stood Solange, Beyoncé, and Jay-Z. The blogosphere could barely process the moment; Solange brought pop music royalty to a free show in Williamsburg. Overnight, Solange became one of the most powerful influencers of the era. Speaking to *Fuse* the day after the show, Jay-Z said of Grizzly Bear: "They were just destroying things and I was like this is it. This is what's gonna happen . . . The indie rock scene right now is in a great place. I enjoy watching it now more than hip-hop."[2] Beyoncé began to seek out more high-profile indie artists, collaborating with Patrick Wimberly and Caroline Polachek (aka indie pop act Chairlift), the singer-songwriter James Blake, and Ezra Koenig from the yacht rock–influenced band Vampire Weekend.

News quickly reached the London punk scene, in which I had recently made my home, and no one was more excited about Beyoncé interacting with indie rock than the punks. Friends would run up to me, barely containing their delusional elation that perhaps Beyoncé would make an indie song. The excitable white punks were clutching at non-existent straws, but so were many other white people in the indie rock scene, who seemed to be desperately on the hunt for the archetypal Black soul diva whose naturally soulful words could sooth a litany of woes. It reminded me of the Black best friend trope in film—you know, the one devoted to the white star, but who is strangely never focused on their own problems. White scenesters wanted to experience Blackness vicariously, using Black artists as positivity cheerleaders to boost them in their lowest moments. In 2019, Lizzo's positive messaging and soulful bops led to success, but also to confusing accusations that she was making music for white people. Though Lizzo is an artist that a certain brand of white feminist has latched on to (even *Mean Girls* creator Tina Fey has shown her love for Lizzo's memeable flute-twerking skills), she has made it clear that no matter who is in her audience, her music is made for a particular ear. "I'm making music that hopefully makes other people feel good and helps me discover self-love. That message I want to go directly to black women, big black women, black trans women. Period."[3] It seems the indie world is always ready for a new Black soul diva to leach from. Back in 2009, it looked like Beyoncé might play that role, but she had the power to bring the indie world to her, so Solange quickly became the replacement. As a result, she experienced the same microaggressions, barely concealed racism, and ignorant remarks as other Black people in the punk and indie rock scene, including me.

In 2009, I volunteered at the community music festival Ladyfest, a punk initiative that promotes women in music and was kick-started by Allison Wolfe, vocalist in the '90s riot grrrl band Bratmobile. After years spent searching for other punks, I saw the London scene as my savior. I threw myself into this new world, organizing events, documenting everything on my music blog, and playing in my first band (a feminist punk five-piece called My Therapist Says Hot Damn), formed when I was twenty-two. At first, I felt at home. The scene's feminist stance aligned with my own nascent political identity, and the people I met welcomed me into their world like an old friend. Despite being on point with queer politics and feminist issues, there was a blindingly obvious problem: the scene was predominantly white, and no one talked about it.

I was one of a handful of people of color in the London punk scene at the time. I would occasionally see Rachel Aggs (the prolific guitarist and singer known for her work in post-punk bands Sacred Paws, Shopping, and Trash Kit) at gigs, but we rarely spoke. Instead we did the same awkward dance around acknowledging each other's presence that so many other people of color engage in daily in majority white spaces. The feeling was that you couldn't possibly draw too much attention to yourself or that your Blackness was ever present. So I and others hid ourselves to stay part of a community that was, at least partially, home. Seeing friends utter racist statements or engage in cultural appropriation was brutal. It was confusing to feel so close to people who had no capacity to relate to such an important part of myself. At practically every punk club night, DJs would play a selection of hip-hop and r&b classics that were old enough to be considered vintage (usually only a decade old) and therefore cool enough for the majority white crowd, who would flood the dance floor, kicking and stomping off-beat. In the middle of those dance floors, I could see the smirks on their faces, the mimicking of dance moves popularized by Black people. They were mocking Black people and using Black culture as their personal costume; it hurt.

During this period, indie rock artists who incorporated traditionally Black genres into their sound began to gain popularity. Though the indie rock world referenced r&b, it was often in an appropriative way, taking elements of the sound while regarding r&b as a genre that did not match the supposed integrity of indie. This pick-and-mix attitude toward other cultures allowed for the majority white, and often middle-class, group of musicians to make a surface-level nod to multiculturalism without unpicking their own privileges. They could reference everything from West African highlife to Afro-Portuguese music in their genre-bounding escapades and be perceived as worldly and mysterious. One could argue that their ability to lift references without fear is due to middle-class economic freedom or the high cultural literacy that can come when you are exposed to wider culture at an early age. In reality, it is simply because white privilege grants itself entry into every room and every space.

The indie band most associated with this debate in recent years is Vampire Weekend. Though the band divided opinions with their African-highlife-meets-yacht-rock style and perceived upper-class privilege (the members met at the Ivy League Columbia University), the group still rose to the top of the charts (their 2008 debut, *Vampire Weekend*, reached number seventeen on Billboard 200). Their consistent use of West African highlife and Congolese pop sounds paired with lyrics about preppy New England life on Cape Cod led critics to declare them the whitest band in the world.[4] It was a criticism that offended them, given the band's mixed heritages (then co-bandleader Rostam Batmanglij's family is Iranian, and lead vocalist Ezra Koenig has pointed to his family's Jewish Romanian heritage). Though the varied immigrant backgrounds of Vampire Weekend are relevant, they don't negate the criticisms about cultural tourism. In a 2019 *Guardian* interview, when asked whether he would still call a song from their debut release "Cape Cod Kwassa Kwassa" today, Koenig suggested that if he had changed the name and adjusted the arrangement, there would have been no outcry, "There's no easy answers, but you have to be thoughtful about it. There's times when criticism helps you to be more thoughtful, and there's times when it's bad-faith clickbait."[5] While Koenig has reflected on the criticism, he still seems prickly about it, suggesting that he believes the critiques were blown out of proportion.

Bringing critical reflection into music is not easy. For the Oakland-based act Tune-Yards (the music project of New

England native Merrill Garbus), reflection became part of their art. The polyrhythmic mashup of Afrobeats, r&b, Haitian music, '80s pop, and punk at the heart of Tune-Yards helped the band top the *Village Voice*'s Pazz and Jop poll with their 2011 album, *Whokill*. Though Garbus rarely faced as much criticism as Vampire Weekend in 2018, she decided to confront her own relationship with appropriation and the debt owed to the creativity of people of color on the album *I Can Feel You Creep Into My Private Life*. It was one example of a white musician attempting to understand how to clearly make out the line between cultural appreciation and appropriation.

Despite the popularity of the indie rock appropriators a decade ago, they rarely sounded as soulful as the artists they were imitating. Enter Solange, who appeared on the landscape with an effortless cover of one of the hottest songs of the year, from Brooklyn's Dirty Projectors, who themselves excelled in their Aaliyah-influenced r&b filtered through quirky pop output. It didn't take much to turn Dirty Projectors' "Stillness Is the Move" into an r&b classic. It basically already was one. The stuttering lead guitar line that composes the main repetitious riff would sound at home anywhere in the illustrious r&b producer Timbaland's lengthy back catalog. Further, lead singer Amber Coffman's syrupy vocals contained the same soft vocal runs and breathy falsetto as Aaliyah in her prime. By sliding in a sample of the guitar lick from "Bumpy's Lament" by Soul Mann and the Brothers—famously sampled by both neo-soul legend Erykah Badu on "Bag Lady" and rapper Dr Dre on "Xxplosive"—Solange took the song to the level it was meant to be heard at. I already loved the lopsided original version, but hearing Solange's angelic vocal interacting with the historic sample felt like she brought "Stillness Is the Move" back home to the Black community that inspired its creation. She received rave reviews from *Village Voice*, and one of the gatekeepers of alternative music at the time, *Pitchfork*. Though the *Pitchfork* reviewer Zach Kelly longed for the other Knowles to tackle this weighty cover (reflecting the indie scene's obsession with seeing Solange as Beyoncé), he did rate the song, stating: "It's a brilliantly sly take on a great song that reflects the malleability of Dirty Projectors' music as well as Solange's impeccable taste."[6] This sign-off from one of the most influential music outlets in the industry forced people to take notice of the woman who was saying, loud and clear to those paying attention, this music right here is mine for the taking, too.

TRUE CONNECTIONS

Solange continued collaborating with a variety of artists, including the Australian band Midnight Juggernauts; her mates Grizzly Bear; the British r&b, dour-pop trio The xx; and the indie pop act Of Montreal. Her new connections would pay off. While working with the Trinidadian American rapper Theophilus London on the track "Flying Overseas," she was introduced to Blood Orange, also known as

Dev Hynes. Raised in Ilford, East London, Hynes entered the music world as a teenager, as Solange did, but in the electro trash emo band Test Icicles. The band's tongue-in-cheek nature and hard-core sound resonated with other teens, but success was short lived, as the band members quickly outgrew their early music. Hynes moved on to a new moniker, Lightspeed Champion, before eventually settling on the stage name Blood Orange and pivoting to a more experimental r&b sound that merged his genre-traversing past.

Solange tried out several producers for her next project (including Pharrell Williams), but Hynes was the perfect match. The pair connected on their mutual appreciation for African percussion, new wave, and '80s r&b. As two Black people who were often the only ones in a room full of white people and were interested in music both within and beyond the realms of what was expected of Black artists, their connection was almost inevitable. On their partnership, Solange said: "This was one of those things where the chemistry was there immediately. It was very natural and second nature for us to create music together."[7] Solange and Hynes worked on the record for two years, producing around thirty songs, spending their first six months together figuring out a cohesive sound that would work for them.

The collaboration became Solange's third release, the EP *True*, released on November 27, 2012. Her love for color theory (the science and art of using color) and Mark Rothko's abstract expressionism inspired the *True* cover, a block-color splash of red, which faded into an ever so slightly warmer tone of red in the lower half of the record. Rothko holds a special place in her heart, as the Rothko Chapel, a nondenominational space in Houston built to house the work of Rothko, was one of the first art spaces outside her home that she was able to visit. Solange used the Rothko Chapel in the dramatic opening shot of her 2019 visual album, *When I Get Home*.

In *True*, Solange wanted to replicate the intricacies and layers of production prevalent in '80s pop, while also showcasing the cohesive sound found when working in close collaboration with one producer. The record, while comprising only seven songs, revived her solo career and became her most critically acclaimed work to date. Released on the independent label Terrible Records, co-run by Grizzly Bear's Chris Taylor, to the industry this was a sign that Solange was truly an indie artist. In reality, in an era when the boundaries between indie and pop began to dissolve due to floundering music markets, major label artists who didn't quite fit in were able to carve out new positions for themselves using indie aesthetics and influences. The pop star Sky Ferreira struggled to get a hit until she also collaborated with Hynes and released the single "Everything Is Embarrassing" in 2012. The downbeat dance pop song revived her career and helped establish her future sound.

Much like Ferreira, Solange worked in the indie arena to control her own destiny, choosing to cowrite and coproduce the record alongside Hynes. Over the course of *True*, the listener is taken on a night of stolen kisses at midnight hang-outs behind the discotheque, and experiences the heartbreak and despondency that follows, exacerbated by the inexperience of youth. The production adds to these effusive displays of after-hours melancholy by using heavily synthesized bass lines, warped vocal samples, and dramatic changes in tone to add to this sullen mood. On "Locked in Closets," the instrumentation moves from jittery, staccato beats to a frenzied wall of synth pop as Solange self-diagnoses her own problems, realizing, "all I wanted was the dream of being in love with you." The record is heavily indebted to the sounds of late '80s pop and is not afraid to wear its influences on its sleeve. While making the record, Solange made a playlist of influences that included the production duo Jimmy Jam and Terry Lewis, known for their work with Janet Jackson and the electro funk S.O.S. Band. To make their '80s kid dreams come true, Hynes and Solange even enlisted the help of Earth, Wind & Fire bassist Verdine White on "Bad Girls (Verdine Version)" to apply a smooth layer of funk to the already groovy song. It is interesting to note that despite Solange and Hynes's Black-centric springboard of ideas, many reviewers likened the '80s influence to early Madonna, perhaps pointing to a lack of diverse experiences and backgrounds in the music media.

With Hynes and Solange working so closely together, their personal lives seeped into the record. Hynes was going through a breakup at the time, and Solange found herself counseling him, providing the female perspective on his relationship. This dynamic can most clearly be seen on the lead single "Losing You," an electro pop fantasy reflecting on a relationship that was destined to fail. Over crackling, midtempo Casio drum machine beats and glitchy looped samples, Solange shifts from mourning over her lost lover to reminding him what actually went down:

I gave you everything and now there's nothing left of me
I'm not the one, that you should be making your enemy

Knowles defiantly tells her soon-to-be ex-lover how she feels, mirroring the tumultuous waves of regret and emotion that come with a breakup. She veers between the bruised partner, sore from recently leaving a relationship (aka Hynes), and the same person further down the line in her life looking back on the past, assured there was nothing more she could have done to save it (Solange).

The video for "Losing You," directed by Melina Matsoukas (known for her work with Beyoncé) was a reflection on Black culture that did not specifically center the African American experience. Solange and her friends traveled to Cape Town, South Africa (courtesy of her mother, who paid for the trip), to celebrate the elegant fashion of Sapeurs. The choice to film the video in South Africa was unusual, as Sapeur culture is actually from the Republic of the Congo. Sapeur or La Sape stands for the Société des Ambianceurs et des Personnes Élégantes (the Society of Tastemakers and Elegant People). In the Congo capital of

Brazzaville, men adopt the mannerisms and style of Parisian colonial dandies with an African twist, donning three-piece pastel suits, canes, and silk handkerchiefs. The style began in the early twentieth century when the French colonized the area. According to the Spanish photographer and filmmaker Héctor Mediavilla, who began documenting the movement in 2003 and directed a 2014 Guinness ad campaign that brought Sapeur culture to TV screens across the world, the movement is about more than style or the postcolonial legacy of their garments. Mediavilla told the UK newspaper the *Telegraph*: "How you treat people is very important. For a man to be a Sapeur he must be gentle, he must not be aggressive, he must be against war, he must be calm tempered."[8]

The Sapeurs stand in opposition to the violence wrought by the colonialism that inspired them. The decadence of these suave gentlemen strolling through neighborhoods is heightened by the reality of their lives. The Republic of Congo has long been mired in the aftermath of war and poverty; according to the World Bank, 41 percent of the population live below the poverty line.[9] Positioning glamour against a backdrop of poverty has become popular in the fashion industry and in the pages of coffee-table books. In fact, Solange stumbled across the Sapeurs while thumbing through the pictorial essay book *Gentlemen of Bacongo*, by the Italian photographer Daniele Tamagni. She was blown away by the culture, describing it as the "most interesting and complex and unique thing that I had seen in a long time."[10] Solange initially tried to film the video in Brazzaville but was told by Tamagni that it would be too expensive and logistically difficult to film in the city. A chance to shoot the cover of *Elle South Africa* and the easier logistics of filming in that country forced Solange to change her plans. Her initial efforts were well intended enough: "We don't want any fake fashion shit, we really want to capture what the vibe is."[11] A Sapeur in London named Dixie told her there was a Congolese Sapeur movement in South Africa and helped find performers for the music video.

The final video is a bustling collage of brightly dressed characters, posing and peacocking as Solange improvises in front of them, swaying from side to side or snapping her fingers, never following an overtly rigorous way of moving. The scenes are intercut with snapshots of life in South African townships as children peer shyly into the camera and elderly women sit casually left of frame in plastic chairs, seemingly oblivious to the filming around them. When I first saw this video, I loved it and thought Solange was highlighting the eccentricity and performative camp that is often central within Black culture.

Some South Africans were annoyed that yet another wealthy US or UK artist used their country as a cool backdrop. Solange does not interact much with the Sapeurs, and other than a few scenes in which she cycles with local children, there is little to suggest the world around her is more than a green screen background. Others questioned why Solange did not feature the South African Swenkas, known for their tailored '40s- and '50s-era suits and popular fashion shows. The website *Africa Is a Country* held a roundtable and asked their staff what they thought about the video. Referencing the Swedish band Little Dragon, which had recently filmed a video in Cape Town, the writer Marissa Moorman claimed that the videos "use these neighborhoods as background, as periphery ghetto chic."[12] The critiques are a reminder that liberatory celebrations of Blackness are not always universal. What Black people in the UK and United States perceive as an attempt to connect with the Black diaspora can feel patronizing and demeaning to Black Africans, who deserve a more meaningful connection than what Black Westerners can take from them.

Despite these critiques, the colorful depictions of Cape Town townships did play well in the United States, and the song "Losing You," along with the EP *True*, was widely praised. In a review for the *Los Angeles Times*, Randall Roberts notes that the EP "delivers seven takes on funky dance music that's smooth without being cheesy, and well-lubricated with solid, snare-driven rhythms."[13] *BBC Music* surmised that the release was an "incredibly addictive pop record that's comparable to no other contemporary release. From a singer who's always been defined by comparisons to somebody else, that's quite an achievement."[14] The praise must have come as a welcome surprise to Solange, who worked hard to ensure the freedom she enjoyed as an independent artist translated to honesty and integrity in her music. So much so that in the early sessions for the EP, she was working around the clock, jeopardizing her mental health. Speaking to *Vibe*, she said: "I can say that I totally sacrificed so much mentally, emotionally and financially to get this record the way I wanted it to be. It's more than an album to me. It's a transitional time in my life."[15] After her struggles to exist within a major label environment, Solange proved she could successfully make it on her own terms. But as the heat from *True* began to die down, it became apparent just what many in the indie scene thought her flirtations with the genre meant and how they would demand penance for her move into a genre they believed was their own.

DON'T BITE THE HAND

Could Solange ever truly cross over into indie? The question rattled around in various insidious guises as review after review noted her hipster stance, unusual style choices, and r&b background. Yet no one thought to ask whether Solange wanted to be seen as an indie star. The answer to that question was no, a stance she was open about from the beginning. Speaking to *Village Voice* back in 2010, Solange said: "They're like, 'Are you going to be this indie-pop girl and be there with your guitar?' And I'm like, 'Hell to the nah!'"[16] She continued: "I left a major label because I didn't like the way it felt to be on one and now I want to be an independent artist. But I don't want this façade of me diving into the indie scene—there's not a conscious effort to that at all."[17]

As a lifelong music nerd, Solange was merely connecting the threads that linked various genres to find the common ground ripe for experimentation. Ironically, it was the same method that brought praise to the feet of her white indie peers, who made a name with their takes on r&b inverted beats. Solange's motives were questioned and overanalyzed rather than accepted as proof of her skill as an experimental musician. Many wondered if it was part of a plot to stand out from the shadow of her sister, who was still one of the world's biggest pop stars. Though the indie scene and her bohemian, "it girl" lifestyle gave her much more freedom than her time as a major label artist had, being independent brought its own set of challenges.

Despite her achievements, Solange was seen as the kooky Black girl who played white music. Her trendy life in Brooklyn led to her becoming an in-demand DJ for exclusive events. Though she sought training from hip-hop pioneer Q-Tip, beat matching for hours on end until she mastered the skill, the terms "DJ" and "hipster" were often thrown at her as slurs. Pretty, female socialite DJs like reality star Paris Hilton often increased their social status and bank balance by DJing at exclusive parties without demonstrating any real skill, so people assumed Solange was just another Paris. In an interview with Hot 97, one of New York's leading hip-hop radio stations, DJ Rosenberg jokingly referred to Solange as a "Brooklyn hipster."[18]

In this use of the word, "hipster" is seen as separate from Black culture. It is connected to white artists, money, and class status. It says you've lost Black points because you spent X amount of time in this arena. Given Hynes's and Solange's statuses (hers, a wealthy, well-connected young Black woman; his, a Black British artist already known for his genre-traversing past), the pair were ripe for ridicule from those who saw them as just trying to be different. During this time, the term "Blipster" (a black hipster) was thrown at any Black person who dared to wear their jeans too tight or sport Day-Glo graphic tees. In a 2009 article from African American online news magazine *The Root*, Dayo Olopade attempts to define the so-called Blipster look: "The racial archetypes that had defined the last 15 years of masculine street style have given way to a radically new aesthetic. Gone are the extra-long T-shirts, saggy jeans and Timbs long favored by young black men. They haven't swapped them for the mopey, emo tees once favored by young whites. Rather, urban youth of all colors now rock snug pants, bright, oversized graphic tees, spotless vanity sneakers and hats with brims flatter than Kansas."[19]

Black people who rocked those flat-brimmed hats and snug pants in the music industry were derided as PBR&B—PBR standing for Pabst Blue Ribbon, a beer associated with hipster culture in the United States. At the time, *True* was lumped in this amorphous grouping. The term was lazily coined (by the creator's own admission) by the music journalist Eric Harvey, who tweeted the sly dig at alt-r&b act

The Weeknd, electronic act How to Dress Well, and Frank Ocean. As Harvey later reflected in an article for *Pitchfork*, the term was reductive for a number of reasons: "I cobbled together three artists who were doing drastically different things, more or less because they were making music that had the capacity to 'cross over,' in old industry parlance. In more modern terms, it's music rooted in African American traditions that . . . well, to put it bluntly, might sell to young white people for whom other types of more rhythm-focused or bluesy modern R&B might not."[20] What I find most unusual about "PBR&B" is that as a term it managed to racialize not just the artists associated with it but also, as Harvey states, the assumed audience as well.

The backlash Black alternative kids receive suggests that society had not yet caught up to the reality that as a generation raised on dial-up internet (as I was), Black artists were well equipped to sift through their multigenre collection of Napster downloaded mp3s to produce a sound that reflected their lives. The idea that indie and r&b are an unusual pairing would fade, along with terms like "PBR&B" and "Blipster" as alternative r&b and the brand Afropunk rose to global prominence. A staple of the live music festival scene now, Afropunk's rise began with a 2003 documentary by the director and punk James Spooner, which sought to capture the lives of Black punks. The documentary *Afro-Punk* was a cult hit and spread across the punk world, lighting up the minds of baby punks like myself when I first watched the film in my university bedroom. In an attempt to create more space for Black punks, Spooner created a message board and then, later in 2005, a small free-to-attend festival in a Brooklyn park. As the festival grew and Spooner became disillusioned with his collaborator Matthew Morgan, he left, and Morgan took the festival even further away from its punk roots toward the burgeoning alternative r&b scene (disclaimer: my band played the London iteration of Afropunk in 2016). The move away from punk (accepting more corporate sponsorships and fewer punk acts, to the disapproval of many Black punks) has technically made the festival more popular than it has ever been, playing host to Solange several times, as well as legendary acts like Grace Jones. The change in Afropunk is seismic and bittersweet. It creates a space for Black eccentricity to thrive, while pushing out Black punks and the radical political activism that went with the festival's original aims.

Solange had bigger problems than being called a hipster. Hynes's input into their collaborative effort was exaggerated to the point that she was seen as his protégé. In *Pitchfork*'s review of *True*, the reviewer claimed: "Hynes has met an ideal female vocal muse in Solange, who executes each cut with simple grace and yearning naïveté."[21] Solange let out her frustration on Twitter: "Y'all got it all the way wrong. I've been writing and producing my own voice since 02, nigga . . . I find it very disappointing when I am presented as the 'face' of my music, or a 'vocal muse' when I write or co-write every fucking song . . . Sexism in the industry ain't nothing new."[22] *True* contained some of her best work to date, but she wasn't getting the credit she deserved for it. On top of that, she was repeatedly profiled as a hipster DJ, fashionista, natural hair movement leader—anything but the musician she was.

Solange's past musical efforts were dismissed as mere whimsy and her new connection with the indie scene was seen as her saving grace. Reporting for the *Village Voice*, the journalist Stelios Phili boldly asked Solange: "You had everyone from Timbaland to Jermaine Dupri producing your debut, *Solo Star*. Do you look back on that record and go, 'Wow, what was I thinking?'"[23] She politely replied that she was proud of her previous efforts, adding, "If people knew how many challenges I dealt with, even to get that product, I think people would've had a more respectable outlook on it."[24] Solange, with her intellect, vast musical knowledge, and pride, was disappointed that so many music journalists couldn't keep up with her. In a 2013 Twitter thread, she said music blogs should employ people who understood the history of hip-hop to write about the genre. She demanded that journalists learn deep cuts from r&b singer Brandy's records if they wanted to appropriately cover r&b albums. Seeing the term "deep cuts"—a phrase most often used in reference to obscure tracks by canonical white male rock stars—used to describe a Black woman's music tickled many journalists, who laughed off Solange's statement.

The ridicule steadily increased. In 2013, on a *New York Times* podcast debating white journalists' role in documenting Black culture, Solange's tweets were mentioned. In response, the writer Jon Caramanica suggested that Solange's popularity was a result of her association with indie acts like Grizzly Bear. "I saw her in concert this year," Caramanica said, "and I felt like a better person when I left the show, but the only reason Solange's success, quote unquote, over the past year has even been a thing is because of the same people she's lambasting. There would be no Solange record if the dude from Grizzly Bear did not put it out. There would be no Solange interest if all of a sudden the people who have historically not been interested in r&b hadn't decided to pay attention to Miguel, The Weeknd, and Drake." He added that Solange should be worried about "not biting the hand that feeds you."[25]

Caramanica's statements insinuated that as a Black woman, Solange needed to refrain from speaking up about the racial disparities she saw unraveling around her if she wanted to please the white people she supposedly needed to keep her career going. The comment hit Solange hard. It stayed with her for years until she finally opened up during her 2016 press tour for *A Seat at the Table*, revealing that moment as the inspiration behind the song "Don't You Wait." In the album liner notes, two whole pages are devoted to the single phrase "bite the hand" as a warning that she won't be silencing herself anytime soon. Speaking about that moment, Solange said: "One of the things that I've explained to the journalist, who has since apologized, was that by him stating that Grizzly Bear made me, who are friends of mine and awesome people and an awesome band, he was being extremely reductive to a lot of people who supported me before *True*, who were young Black people. What he was basically trying to say is that even though *Sol-Angel and the Hadley St. Dreams* actually reached more people from a numerical point of view than *True*, I am only relevant to him because the people who he aligns himself with are saying that I'm relevant."[26]

Caramanica's comment was representative of the microaggressions Solange and other people of color in the indie rock scene have to endure. It is a system designed to keep you in your place, that says you're lucky to have white people love your music, as if the number of white listeners can be a marker for good taste. It kept Black creatives downtrodden and ignores the racism in the scene. This bigotry dressed up in progressive clothing started to eat at me, too. How many times could I be mistaken for the other Black girl in the bar? How many times can I be told to be grateful for what I have until I realize I don't need them and could create something of my own?

Solange has described her time in the indie scene as traumatic, but it was pivotal for her progression as an artist. After years of contorting herself to fit into other scenes, through her experiences during the *True* era she realized the only way to fully excel as the artist she longed to be was to create space for herself. She went away and started Saint Heron (a cultural hub celebrating art, music, and design) and Saint Records. Her venture would create a new space for up-and-coming artists who were as unconventional as she was. The cultural hub was a success, and Saint Heron played a part in the early careers of alt-r&b's Kelela and Sampha, a South London producer and Solange collaborator on *A Seat at the Table* and *When I Get Home*. If the white music press wanted to know what biting the hand that feeds them is like, she was going to give it to them.

As Solange was cultivating her Black millennial collective, I was still in London playing in a majority white feminist punk band. I realized my dream was to create a Black punk band and a space for other Black punks. It's a strange coincidence, but we both decided, "fuck this life" and started something new. My incentive to center myself more in my music came one day in 2013 when I saw a short post on social media asking people to form new bands for an event called First Timers, a gig where every band plays their first show. I posted on Facebook asking if anyone would want to join a Black punk band. Chardine, whom I had met a few months prior at a Black feminist meeting, responded immediately. When I forgot to send a reply, she DMed me with her vision for the band and (importantly for the future of Big Joanie) her wish to play drums standing up like her heroes, the Scottish shoegaze band the Jesus and Mary Chain. We found our original bassist, Kiera Coward-Deyell, online as well, declared ourselves a Black feminist sistah punk band, and worked furiously on our set of half original songs and half covers. The name Big Joanie is my ode to my mum Joan and a play on the way the Jamaican community uses the term "big" to mean adult or grown up. Big Joanie to me is a phrase that connotes a strong, confident woman. As we prepared for the upcoming First Timers gig in rehearsal rooms all over London, we developed the familial gang mentality that so often happens with bands. Looking over at my band mates as we chatted about our lives and the world around us, I knew the magic of the band arose in those moments when, secluded from the outside world, we, as three Black women, could truly be ourselves away from the oppressive conformity of mainstream society. The beauty of Big Joanie lies in the ideas that can be created in moments when Black women, momentarily, feel free.

Over the years, the topic of starting a punk festival for people of color in the UK came up in our band practices. As time went on, the band forgot about it, but I still badly wanted the festival to exist. What would happen if we took the security the band brought us and applied it to a festival setting? Taking inspiration from DIY festivals in the United States for punks of color, like Chicago's Black and Brown Punk Fest, I decided to see if anyone in London was up for our own version. I asked my friends on social media what bands they'd want to see at a punks of color festival, and the response was overwhelming. The South London punk venue DIY Space for London wanted me to book the venue before I'd even committed to organizing the festival. Building on this excitement, a gang of punks of color met, and we created Decolonise Fest. At the first event, held over three days in June 2017, we hosted workshops and panels during the day on intersectional resistance in the punk scene and grassroots activists of color. In the evening, bands like the noise metal two-piece Divide and Dissolve and the Glaswegian art pop band Sacred Paws took to the stage demanding that punks of color storm to the front of the stage.

The festival was a success. Throughout the weekend, audience members approached me and other collective members to express their excitement and divulged their personal stories of feeling disconnected from the punk scene. We have held the annual festival ever since, building community and spreading the word about the history of punks of color. In Decolonise we are giving people of color who may not have felt like they had a place in the punk scene a space where, for a weekend, they are the priority. We take over white punk venues and convert them into spaces filled with people of color, where we can bring our culture, our food, and our full selves. We engage in radical organizing and show festival goers how they can get involved in political action. This is all done in the hope that someone goes home from the festival with the radical words of our bands in their head, sees the inequalities in their community, and thinks, "I can stop this."

While Decolonise Fest and Big Joanie were my contributions to the changing music scene, the catalyst for my projects was bigger than just myself or my music scene. One of the most important activist movements of this generation,

Black Lives Matter, was coming to life and would inspire many ordinary people to take a stand. Solange and I, like the rest of the Black community, couldn't help but get involved and be inspired. The seeds of our future lay in our hands. All we had to do was cultivate them, nurture them, and reclaim what was rightfully ours.

— 5 —

ROOTING FOR EVERYBODY BLACK

During the summer of 2013, tucked away in an unassuming Long Island studio, Solange began crafting the underlying sonic landscape of *A Seat at the Table*. The record was her chance to reconnect with her ancestors and continue her personal journey toward self-discovery. She wanted to become a better mother, wife, and sister to her family but first needed to unravel a few home truths. As she dug deep, she began connecting her anger, depression, and mental health with more expansive meditations on the Black experience in America. She took her writing and recording process around the world, to New Iberia, New Orleans, Brooklyn, Ghana, and Jamaica. Solange mined her A-list connections and wide-ranging music tastes to bring together an eclectic group of musicians and producers. She wanted to collaborate with veterans, like the r&b producer Raphael Saadiq, as well as relative newcomers, such as the British singer-songwriter Kindness. She would be led by the wisdom of her elders while staying rooted in the contemporary sounds of the younger generation. The pianist and composer Ray Angry was pulled into an early session by the drummer Questlove, known for his work in the hip-hop band the Roots. Along with the UK alt-r&b artist Sampha and Solange herself, the group jammed along to her song ideas. Even in those early stages, Angry was stunned by Solange's artistry: "I remember leaving the studio and her saying, 'Oh, man, you're like really a genius,' but then I was thinking, 'Shit, *you're* a fucking genius.' I remember thinking, man, what just happened?"[1]

Solange left an impression on many of the musicians she worked with. In New Orleans, she brought a group of musicians of color from the UK into her studio and spent ten days fleshing out song ideas. Olugbenga Adelekan, the bassist in the electro-indie band Metronomy, was part of that group. Sometimes Solange would leave the musicians alone to give them space to create, returning later to hone their day's work. Adelekan felt Solange chose the musicians in order to create a unique space where whiteness was the minority—the only white person present during those sessions was the engineer Mikaelin "Blue" BlueSpruce—to change the dynamics of the working environment. "I think for all of us it was very interesting for us to be in a room with basically all Black or mixed-race people working on an album," Adelekan said. "Because I mostly do indie rock–type stuff, it was quite an unusual setting for me to be in. It seems to me that it was quite a self-conscious decision on her part, because it kind of timed with all the stuff she seemed to be into and the places she was showing us in New Orleans, which is like different sides of the Black culture, and the southern Black culture specifically, which as people who lived in England, we're maybe gonna be less familiar with it, and there was a feeling that she wanted to show that to us."[2]

Solange's tutorial on southern Black culture came mostly via walks around the New Orleans neighborhood where the studio was located and trips to indulge in traditional southern food. The group ate and discussed the Black diaspora and how Black American culture is often seen in a different light outside of the United States. It is true that the UK's vision of Black American culture is filtered through hip-hop, fashion trends, social media, and historical references to the civil rights movement. There is rarely a chance to understand the culture beyond those narratives. Later during the group's stay in New Orleans, Solange suggested that they visit the Angola Prison Rodeo in Baton Rouge, a "fair meets friends and family day" for prisoners, stating the event was "one of the most southern things that you're ever gonna go to."[3] Uncomfortable at first, the group eventually settled into the event, watching the rodeo with the rest of the crowd and perusing the prisoners' handmade crafts on sale. At times, the group had to remind themselves they were at a prison and not a state fair.

The chilling juxtaposition of watching the prisoners take part in what should be a fun event, while knowing Angola has a majority Black population and is situated on a former plantation, was hard for Adelekan to take in as an outsider. Looking back on the event, he thinks,

"That was something where she was overtly wanting to show us something almost quite dark, weird—but also in the midst of that, people were joking and having a good time," Adelekan muses. "It's kind of like the complexity of a certain side of the Black American experience, I guess."[4] Taking into account Solange's show-and-tell around New Orleans, their conversations on Black American culture, and the fact that she recorded the album in other majority Black countries (Jamaica and Ghana), Adelekan believes Solange wanted the "input of different experiences of Blackness."[5] This allowed her to create a vision of Blackness that took into account experiences that may not have married with her own but still regard them as equal.

Released on September 30, 2016, through her label Saint Records and Columbia Records, *A Seat at the Table* is Solange's meditation on Black pride, the Black experience, and self-acceptance seen through the eyes of a young African American woman. Following in the footsteps of radical Black artists turned activists, such as the high priestess of soul Nina Simone or the Motown legend Marvin Gaye, with *A Seat at the Table* Solange created a time capsule for her generation. The record discusses radical softness, healing as a revolutionary act, Black womanhood, and generational trauma. It does so without being marred by tired slogans or a self-pitying narrative. In full motivational speaker mode, Solange reminds the Black community to step into their light and recognize their wounds for what they are and declares that they are strong enough to carry on. Her voice had developed immensely since her early releases, now able to conjure the sweet delights of artists like the iconic r&b singer Minnie Riperton while still possessing the individuality that sets her apart from other artists. *A Seat at the Table* is an amalgam of hazy funk, distilled r&b, plush horns, and downtempo disco, but through Solange's confident delivery, the audience is never left considering whether the record belongs in any one category. While many view *A Seat at the Table* as a companion record to Beyoncé's *Lemonade* (2016), released a few months prior, to me, Solange's record stands apart, with its own message and unique delivery. Critical reception to the album was overwhelmingly positive and reasserted Solange as a distinguished artist with a singular voice. It became her first number-one album on the Billboard 200 in the United States, all while speaking to the Black community she held dearly.

ON BLACKNESS

A Seat at the Table tells the story of the Black experience with as much authenticity and accuracy as one project can. While the album does not aim to have the final word on what defines Blackness, it does bring in multiple voices—including her parents and the founder of No Limit Records, rapper Master P—to ensure the album represents other perspectives. Master P came to the studio at first to record an interlude to "F.U.B.U." (For Us, By Us). "I asked him to come in and speak for this one song, and he ended up being the most incredible storyteller. We ended up talking for an hour and a half, two hours. It was so natural and it was, literally, like being in a self-help seminar."[6] To Solange, he represented the pinnacle of Black empowerment and independence that her father had preached to her for years. She realized she needed to make his role on the album more prominent.

After spending years working on the album, Solange was tired and exhausted with the process. Master P's speech, covering everything from self-belief, financial independence, and the refusal to revere whiteness, revitalized her enthusiasm for the project. To keep the conversation going, Solange asked him to comment on each track, imagining Master P would become the MC easing the listener into the vibe of each song. In the end, his original conversations would be used sporadically throughout the album, to connect with the tone of each song they either follow or precede. Following the celebratory anthem "Don't Touch My Hair," Master P confidently preaches on "This Moment," explaining, "If you don't understand us and understand what we've been through, then you probably wouldn't understand what this moment is about. This is home. This is where we from. This is where we belong." A riotous horn section accompanies the beginning of his speech as if to underline the importance of what is being said. Master P is a crucial narrator in the story *A Seat at the Table* aims to tell. His voice and experience as an older Black father figure communicated the ingrained sense of self-motivation and political awareness Solange saw in the Black community.

When I listen to Master P, I hear the encouraging words of my uncles when they take me aside and tell me how proud they are of me. I hear common-sense advocation for hard work and discipline from my dad. I hear the reminder my grandad regularly gave my mum that as Black people, this world won't give us anything for free, so take what you can and run.

While Master P's interludes bring to mind an older generation passing down wisdom to the next, the interlude "I Got So Much Magic, You Can Have It" is about Black millennial women speaking to one another. The snippet is an a cappella celebration of the beauty of Black women. Solange is joined by the LA-based soul singer Nia Andrews and Kelly Rowland to joyfully remind us, "Don't let anybody steal your magic, yeah / But I got so much y'all." The twenty-six-second track is an infectiously heartening display of Black girl magic. The trio giggles and laughs about the majesty inherent in them—so much of it they're willing to give a little away to those who need it. Their proclamations run over into the beginning of "Junie," a song about cultural appropriation and the misuse of Black culture. The conversation around Black girl magic was at its peak in 2016, with numerous articles trying to decipher the affirmative phrase. Black girl magic is one of a number of positive phrases (such as "Black joy" or "Black boy joy") coined to celebrate Black culture and people in a world that often overlooks Black people. Solange's play on Black girl magic reaffirms her intention to center Black women's experiences. Though Black women play around with the positive terms, Solange, like many in the Black community, understandably has a conflicted relationship with these terms. Speaking to *Fader* magazine, she said: "In one sense, it's incredibly difficult that we even have to come up with the term 'Black joy,' to identify that as a state of mind. We should just be able to exist whenever and however we please and choose to. But I also understand the power of manifesting something when you speak it into existence, and almost needing to give it a name to show people, 'Hey, this is how we see ourselves and this is how we want you to see us.'"[7]

Both Master P's speeches and "I Got So Much Magic . . ." are crucial building blocks in the narrative of the Black community Solange is building; another important addition is voiced by Solange's parents. By the time Solange asked her parents to record their now cherished interludes a few months before the album was released in 2016, the record was already complete. Solange did not tell her parents they would be in a room together, a surprise for the ex-couple, who had not seen each other since their divorce in 2011. The pair broke through the initial surprise and engaged in an open conversation with their daughter. Solange's determination to speak to her parents, especially her father, was inspired by an uncommonly talkative therapist Solange had been seeing. In an effort to tackle the piercing rage Solange so often found herself succumbing to, she sought out the same therapist as her father, who revealed that one of the topics he spoke about was racial trauma. As a daughter who saw her father intermingling in white corporate America every day, and who at first glance seemed to have overcome so much, Solange was surprised and wondered if her father's racial trauma had been passed down to her.

On "Dad Was Mad," Mathew Knowles reflects on the day he had to desegregate a white school as a child while angry mobs and the vicious KKK swarmed around him, engulfing him in their hatred. He remains stoic as he tells his story, but what extra flourish of emotion is needed when recalling the moment you truly feared for your life? The stark reality of his story is undercut by light, peppy piano notes that escalate in their playful nature as the interlude continues. The deliberate juxtaposition draws the listener's attention even closer to his story. It also offers a sense of optimism in the joyful bursts of piano, denoting that all is not lost. In the liner notes for her album, Solange thanks her parents for "getting mad, and then deciding getting mad wasn't enough, and building brick by brick for us to walk the pavement proudly."[8] Like Solange, her parents used their anger to forge a path for themselves without forgetting about it or why it was there.

Tina's interlude presents the proud Black woman both Solange and Beyoncé have always paid homage to. Tina has no qualms about her Blackness or how she sees herself. She talks about the beauty of Black people and segues seamlessly into breaking down how ridiculous the concept of "reverse racism" is and the ways white culture suppresses

Black pride. The powerful speech drives home the feeling of optimism and triumph Solange vowed to leave the listener with. Solange has stated that all the speakers she chose expressed feelings she could not at the time, but she singles out her mother's speech as the most positive interlude. So much so that while recording she had to stifle yelps of agreement when her mother made a particularly astute point. The use of other voices, other experiences, and her family members is as important as the music itself because it allows the album to break free from the standard format to function as an archive for the generations. By centering other voices and stories, Solange shows that this album truly is for and by Black people.

The urge to center Black voices fits within the many demands for Black representation that have become ubiquitous in all aspects of culture. When I try to summarize the whirlwind of Black power the world has become caught up in in recent years, my mind always drifts to a remark by the star and creator of the hit HBO series *Insecure*, Issa Rae. When asked who she wanted to win at the 2017 Emmy Awards, Rae replied: "I'm rooting for everybody Black."[9] Her off-the-cuff quip became a memeable quote, demonstrating how Black solidarity and community is essential to the manifestation of Black pride. As well as giving space on the record to those she respected most, Solange used a variety of methods to show Black solidarity and reflect the breadth of the Black experience. Speaking to NPR in 2016, she said: "I think that honestly while writing the record, I was writing for myself, to be honest. I was writing for my family and my friends. I was wanting to be the voice of my group text chat. I was wanting to be the voice of my grandparents. I was wanting to be the voice of my son, my niece. So I think that's really the audience that I was writing from the perspective of. Some songs are received in a certain way, but I honestly was writing them for myself and for my healing and for my self-discovery. On some moments, that can be universal. And then some moments, I feel like that is for us, by us, and we deserve to have that moment."[10] Her dedication to reflecting the thoughts of her loved ones led to friends and family listening to the album prior to its release, rejigging the track listing in relation to their reactions until she felt the record sonically flowed with everyone's story.

Much like Rae's quote, *A Seat at the Table* instantly became a part of Black culture, popping up as memes on Black Twitter (a collective identity used to describe the way Black users interact on the social media site) and the group chats of many Black friendship groups. The existential despair of "Cranes in the Sky" was hilariously captured by a series of posts featuring a Kermit the Frog puppet enacting every line. Other memes focus on the iconic image of the album cover, where Solange looks defiantly at the camera with a transitional hairstyle, wearing those multi-colored clips found at every Black hairdressers. While the artwork itself is important because it epitomizes the traumatic themes of the album, the image has come to represent the humor found in Black millennial inertia and despair of everyday life. The character D.W. (Dora Winifred) from the popular animated series *Arthur* (beloved in the Black community and seen as a representation of the Black family by some) is transformed into Solange with a weary look on her face. In another meme, Solange is merged with the popular "everything is fine" image, placing a cartoon Solange in a room ablaze, unaware of the literal and emotional danger she is in. Twitter user Gabi Thorne pairs the image with the tweet "I tried to meme it away, I tried to post it on twitter. . . ."[11] The meme conveys the tongue-in-cheek way Black millennial Twitter uses humor to get through anxiety-inducing moments that often seem overwhelming. That the term Black Twitter is so ubiquitous demonstrates the power in the way Black people communicate. Solange's ability to sway conversations on Black Twitter illustrates how embedded she is in the culture.

The Black community is also evoked in the album's title, *A Seat at the Table*. The phrase is often used to depict marginalized communities being given a chance to wield the same power and influence as the privileged elite. Sheryl Sandberg, Facebook COO and author of *Lean In: Women, Work, and the Will to Lead*, has used the term in reference to women in business, telling women to "sit at the table" if they want to succeed in the workplace.[12] Sandberg's use of the term is a liberal feminist approach to representation politics, which does not account for what table these women will be sitting at. If a company profits from the oppression of marginalized people, would it make much difference if one of the employees was a woman?

For the academic and author Melissa Harris-Perry, the term a "seat at the table" refers to the ways in which Black women have tried to usurp political power. Over Skype, Harris-Perry uses the example of Shirley Chisholm, the first Black woman elected to the US Congress and the first Black woman to seek a major party's nomination for president of the United States. "If you say 'a seat at the table,' that's Shirley Chisholm, right? Shirley Chisholm literally saying, "If they won't give you a seat at the table, bring a folding chair," right? And here, in Ohio, the woman who was sworn to the city council and literally brought a folding chair. It's like my favorite thing that happened."[13] The politician Harris-Perry was referencing was Cincinnati city councilwoman Tamaya Dennard, who wore a Shirley Chisholm pin and brought a red folding chair to her swearing-in ceremony while promising to serve her community.

The meaning of the phrase "a seat at the table" changes as the album unfolds. Solange imagined outsiders pulling up a chair to learn more about Black culture. It is also a way for a plethora of cultures to unite, listen, and learn from one another. Considering the Black feminist message at the core of the album, I can't help but draw parallels with Kitchen Table: Women of Color Press, cofounded by the Black feminist scholar Barbara Smith in 1980 (at the request of her friend poet and scholar Audre Lorde) to publish the work of women of color. When asked why they chose the name "Kitchen Table," Barbara Smith stated: "We chose our name because the kitchen is the center of the home, the place where women in particular work and communicate with each other."[14] Using the table—where Black people are loved, eat, and celebrate—as a unifier, Solange is following in the footsteps of Black feminists, reasserting the importance of good food, communication, and love in the Black community.

WRITING US INTO EXISTENCE

Writing about Blackness without accidentally rendering the identity into a monolith is difficult. Many have tried to document aspects of Black identity that seem universal, or tell their personal journey, whether it aims to be political or not. As Nina Simone memorably uttered, "an artist's duty . . . is to reflect the times," and Solange was not alone in her aspirations to speak to her community.[15] Kendrick Lamar's *To Pimp a Butterfly* (2015) utilized jazz stylings, funk, spoken word, and unconventional song structures to speak on the brutality of police violence and the Black experience. Kendrick inspired everyone from David Bowie to Black Lives Matter protesters, who used his song "Alright" as a defiant rallying call to keep spirits up at protests. Beyoncé's *Lemonade* (2016) explored the power of Black female rage, the immense pain caused by infidelity, and the ways in which Black women can heal. In 2014, the neo-soul legend D'Angelo came back from a fourteen-year hiatus with *Black Messiah*, released early in response to the Ferguson,

Missouri, riots that erupted after the fatal shooting of a Black teenager, Michael Brown, by the police, bringing hope to a distressed community.

Given that many have tried and succeeded, it also has to be acknowledged that many have tried and failed. As the reality of racial and social inequalities became ever present in the minds of a generation that came of age following protests and educating themselves on social media, more entertainers tried to crowbar messaging into their work that did not always match up to the art created. In *The Cut*, the writer Molly Fischer argues that pop culture's great "awakening," as she calls it, has led to a climate in which it is impossible to discuss contemporary pop culture without determining whether it is sufficiently woke. This turning point, as revolutionary as it can be, has not automatically led to great art: "An artist can be so perfectly attuned to the moment that he or she makes machines precision engineered to flatter contemporary taste. An artist can also be so perfectly attuned to the moment that he or she sees what's unsaid and so says something new. The first category is disposable; the second is not. The work of a critic—alert to ideals, alert to ambition—is to tell the difference."[16] Knowing how to be creatively attuned to the moment, as Fischer states, takes a lifetime for many artists. I believe Solange has achieved this through her long career, her family's pride in the Black community, and her dedication to staying true to herself. Questions of political authenticity have not arisen for Solange, perhaps because she has frequently spoken about the racial micro-aggressions in her career and everyday life. Both the song "Weary" and the essay *And Do You Belong? I Do*, released a few weeks prior to the album, tackle the overwhelming inertia felt when confronted with the drip, drip of every-day racism.

The essay discusses how racism is often delivered in a dismissive tone, using blunt language. "Many times the tone just simply says, '*I do not feel you belong here.*'"[17] On a night out with her family to see Kraftwerk, a group of white women sitting behind Solange expressed to her, in this similar tone, that she did not belong. When Solange started dancing in front of them in a seated area, the women yelled and threw trash at her when her back was turned. In her recollections of that night, Solange runs through every stage in the cycle of emotions racism inflicts on Black peo-ple: disbelief it is happening, anger, bottling of said anger because you've been taught to cater to white emotions, the impression you're alone in your situation, a need to tell your truth, and the eventual despair you're left with when you tell your story and no one believes you. "Weary" docu-ments that cycle. In the confusion and loneliness, sparks of power are fired up, fueled by her search for her "body" and "glory." The song opens with a subdued bass line that dominates the instrumentals, backed by a steady drum pat-ter, while short bursts of keys repetitively rise and fall. Sol-ange's hushed vocals are almost at the point of whisper as she carefully expresses her state of mind:

I'm weary of the ways of the world
I'm going look for my body yeah
I'll be back real soon

Solange speaks to her exhaustion at the never-ending cycle of everyday racism; from the low-level hum of the sideways glances in white neighborhoods to the siren-level scream of racial violence. It all melds into one all-consuming wall of fear that often feels impossible to overcome, rendering the feeling of weariness. Her search for her "body" is in tune with mindfulness (which Solange has mentioned she practices to help her feel centered) that helps calm anxiety. She states that she is going back to the body, an important practice in mindfulness that involves stopping to focus on your body, on what is hurting and why. One must make time to master this process, taking a break from the world to understand yourself and thus be reminded of your humanity. In turn, Solange also seeks her "glory," the positive attributes that define her. The repetitive refrain of "I'll be back real soon" is a reminder that though she has a difficult journey ahead, she will make it back to herself and back to center. The answer to her questions seems to be succinctly surmised in Master P's interlude, which flows easily after "Weary" and confirms, "Everybody is always talking about peace, but, as long you find peace in what you doing then you successful, and that's what people don't realize. See, you got do stuff till where you can go sleep at night. 'Cause the glory is, is in you."

"Weary" is quietly rebellious in its aim to free a Black woman from the weight of societal pressures and its conclusion that power comes from within. It was the first song that stood out to me from the album, which likely speaks to the forever-teenage emo that lurks inside me. After I first listened to the album, I found myself singing "Weary" while waiting in line at the supermarket or sitting alone in a half-empty train carriage staring out the window. As much as I like feeling sorry for myself, "Weary" does not leave me under the same gray cloud as the emo bands I used to love. A ray of positivity and grit shines through as Solange speaks to the humanity of Black people, but it is not a plea for understanding:

> But you know that a king is only a man
> With flesh and bones, he bleeds just like you do
> He said "Where does that leave you"
> And do you belong? I do

Often in response to oppression there is a pressure from wider society that you must appeal to the better nature of one's oppressor, remind them you are flesh and blood, that this knife hurts, that words leave scars. Many marginalized people have come to believe that we cannot appeal to the better nature of an oppressor whose version of morality does not make space for marginalized people's lived experience. Instead of appealing directly to the white gaze, "Weary" tells a story of white dismissal to its audience of Black listeners, knowing that sometimes Black people can only trust ourselves to be witness to our own truths. Though Black people are still weary, the song ends with an affirmation pointing to a better future, because even in the midst of everything that happens, we still know we do belong. And if we belong, we deserve better.

Once we determine we deserve better, we must decide how we reach that goal. "Where Do We Go" documents the story of a community stuck in a moment. Afraid of the past and the place they came from, they face a future that is also uncertain. The song is in part a tribute to Solange's grandparents' journey to Texas after they were run out of their small hometown in Louisiana. She opens with a revealing insight into how many families running away from terror have to move:

Speakers off tonight
Turn off your headlights tonight
Don't drive the road too slow
Don't look too close tonight

Traveling in fear, they make no noise, draw no attention to themselves, never look back, foot on the gas pedal because they don't want to get caught. Her family's story reflects the African American community's search for a better future, from the "conquer and divide" tactics of colonialism as implied in the second verse, to modern day, where, due to the prevalence of racial violence, it can often feel as if Black people are still running. It is not just a physical place Solange speaks of but a mentality. Speaking directly to the Black community, she asks: Where do "we" want to be? How do "we" build a better future? How do "we" recognize it when we reach it?

The instrumentals add to the solemn nature of the song, from the tinkling piano keys to the heavy slap of the hi-hat and snare at the start of each beat. The Canadian singer-songwriter Sean Nicholas Savage helped work on the song, adding his lo-fi approach to production: "She kept it super raw in the end, and I was delighted about that! The beat got way more smashed, and I loved that, too."[18] As the song fades out, the promise of a brighter future hangs in the air. We do not get to find out where we go from here, there are no answers for now, only questions for Black listeners to ponder. The answers may not come tomorrow, but if we are to go by the triumphant instrumentals that close the song, those answers will manifest soon enough.

The present environment Solange wants to escape from so desperately in "Where Do We Go" is evident in "Don't You Wait" and "Junie," two songs that discuss the microaggressions of all-white environments. Both songs recall Solange's experience of the indie rock scene. Her interaction with the writer Jon Caramanica, when he told her not to bite the hand that feeds her by criticizing the indie scene, has been immortalized in "Don't You Wait" with a steely response:

Now, I don't want to bite the hand
that'll show me the other side
But I didn't want to build the land
That had fed you your whole life
Don't you find it funny

Solange sat on her feelings for years following her skir-
mish with Caramanica. His comment asked her to be silent,
and in return, the predominantly white indie rock scene
would reward her with the veneration it believes it controls
and can bestow. Here she reminds Caramanica, and other
white people who lazily view indie rock as a superior genre
of music, that the world they believe they own was actually of her own making. Indie rock, of course, is rooted
in the inventive rock 'n' roll of Black musicians. America,
the land white people see as their birthright, was stolen
from Indigenous people and fed its white citizens from
fields sown by the slave labor of African people, and the
railways connecting the vast country were built by East
Asian labor. The United States as it exists now, as with
much of modern music, has not been built by white hands
alone. In this moment in the song, Solange gives hope
to everyone who ever wanted to clap back at their arch-
nemesis but couldn't summon a witty-enough response in
the moment. In a cool, assured tone delivered over subtle, repetitive beats that brush aside the barbed speech of
white privilege, Solange tells the white crowd from her

True days just what she thinks about them. She knows if she returns to that place, the same people will still be there "still looking for nothing," still not seeing her for who she truly is. She proclaims she'll be better off without them and goes on her way.

"Junie" takes aim at flagrant acts of cultural appropriation, which is defined as the adoption of elements of one culture by members of another culture to negative effect. The most referenced examples include white festival-goers wearing Native American headdresses, and white pop stars, like Katy Perry, wearing cornrows or performing in a Japanese geisha-inspired outfit. The song title "Junie" was inspired by the funk musician Junie Morrison, who wrote and produced for the Ohio Players and Parliament-Funkadelic. It was Morrison's song "Super Spirit," a soaring, greasy funk track, that caught Solange's attention. Along with Morrison, on "Junie" and throughout the album, I can also hear the influence of the inventive neo-soul doyenne Erykah Badu, whom Solange has named as one of her influences on numerous occasions. There are very few places in contemporary r&b where the influence of Badu's incense-scented soul cannot be found. Ever since her debut *Baduizm*, released in 1997 to critical and commercial acclaim, Badu, along with her neo-soul contemporaries (Jill Scott, D'Angelo, and Angie Stone, to name a few), revived the spirit of early '70s funk, incorporating her own themes of spiritualism and individuality. On "Junie," Solange talks of returning home "free from the mother mind," a spiritual turn of phrase that would sound at home any-where in Badu's back catalog. The song is at points confron-tational and almost humorous in nature, pointing out the hypocrisy of appropriation by using examples:

> You want to be the teacher
> Don't want to go to school
> Don't want to do the dishes
> Just want to eat the food

Here, Solange leaves no room for appropriation to be valid. It is as ridiculous as being an uneducated teacher or a lazy dinner guest who doesn't want to pitch in at the end of an evening. The line gives listeners a peek into the per-sonality of Solange. Her use of humor is a practice Badu was also able to weave into her work. The most notable moment came on her *Live* album, released in 1997, where she debuted her scathing takedown of useless partners, "Tyrone." In her requests for her man to "call Tyrone" to help him get his things and out of her life, Badu employs colloquial phrases used by the African American commu-nity to drive home her comedic point. She reminds her man "you don't never buy me nothin'" and whenever they go out, she has to "pay your way and your homeboys' way and sometimes your cousin's way." It is a slick, storytelling motif that Badu and Solange use to declare that they are predominantly speaking to a certain audience. Despite the humor, "Junie" ends on a query for us to ruminate over:

But what you gonna do when they saw all your moves
and practiced 'em daily?
Protect your neck or give invitations?

Solange asks if we acknowledge cultural appropriation for what it is, how should we deal with the issue? Do we separate ourselves, protect our culture to protect ourselves, or allow others to take part in our culture, giving guidance in the hope they will pay homage with respect? Culture has always been a porous state, with blurred boundaries that leak from one group to another, often without anyone being overtly aware that it is happening. It is this natural exchange that can lead to the creation of something entirely new, such as an exchange that lit the rebellious energy of the London punk scene through the anti-establishment reggae music the punks loved, or prompted Detroit's all-Black rock band Death to combine the classic rock style of the Who with their funk background to create proto-punk, years before punk fully kicked off. Of course, for cultural exchange to be successful, one must give back in order to receive, a point many in privileged positions should heed.

In "Junie" and across the rest of *A Seat at the Table*, Solange writes into canon the feeling of release when you finally stumble across the words that bring to life the reality you've always lived. It is the power that comes from storytelling, sharing, and consciousness raising. It is the self-belief one gains after seeing others who can help you toward safety and prosperity, giving you the confidence to take the lead and become the guide for others, once your education is sufficient. It is the fire bubbling underneath that inspires you to finally make change.

— 6 —

CREATING COMMUNITY

In my early twenties, I could never claim to be anything other than consistently meek. Naturally reserved, I wielded my shyness like a shield to keep a barrier between me and my surroundings, which constantly baffled me. I moved from being the only Black girl in my friendship group at school, to the only Black girl at university, graduating to be known as the only Black girl in my post-student-life friendship group. While the scenery changed, the problems remained the same. My acquaintances casually discussed how Black women should be grateful to white feminists, for what reason I am still unsure. Some made tongue-in-cheek racist jokes, unaware that to live in the leftist utopia they dreamed of, they would have to stick to all of the principles. Every time I encountered these indiscretions, I would be incensed inside. When you are the target of racism, your first thought is to run away and pretend it isn't happening, but if it surrounds your immediate environment, there's nowhere to run. I wanted to speak up, to scream and cry, but when I opened my mouth to tell my truth, the words would snag in my throat. It wasn't just the racism that angered me, it was the fact that people cared so little about me that they did it in front of my face. I knew I needed to be around people who could relate to the nonsense I was putting up with, but my shyness made it hard to make new friends.

I stopped capitulating to racism when I was twenty-two. It was 2010, I was just about to start my first job in journalism and bashfully joined my first punk band. That's when I found out about Black Feminists, a monthly meeting group for women of color in London. Based on the feminist activist method of consciousness raising, first used in the mid-1960s, we took turns discussing our lives and discovered we were experiencing similar problems. By connecting the dots, we, as fellow group member and bestselling author Reni Eddo-Lodge wrote, "took what we thought were isolated incidents, and lined them into a broader context of race and gender."[1]

Through the group, I made lasting and deep connections with other Black women. They pushed me to strive for more in every aspect of my life, nurtured my budding activist mindset, and vastly improved my sense of self. Black Feminists saw ourselves in the lineage of similar groups of the '70s and '80s, such as the Brixton Black Women's Group and the Organisation of Women of African and Asian Descent (OWAAD), who created a radical, educational, activist collective. It is worth noting that these women did not identify as a consciousness-raising group, viewing the idea as a luxury they did not have time for, considering the pressing inequalities they were coping with.

With Black Feminists, we created what bell hooks would call a community of resistance, based on the Buddhist monk Thich Nhat Hanh's teachings that "communities of resistance should be places where people can return to themselves more easily, where the conditions are such that they can heal themselves and recover wholeness."[2] Hooks argues that, traditionally, Black women were crucial to creating such communities, which were the backbone of political movements: "Working together to build communities that foster a sense of kinship that goes beyond blood ties or bonds of friendship, Black women expand our horizons. When communities of resistance are everywhere the norm in our lives, we will not be without a circle of love or a healing place. Such communities of resistance can emerge around our struggles for personal self-recovery as well as our efforts to organize collectively to bring about social change."[3] The possibility to make active change by connecting with Black women who big you up all day long has been an integral part of my growth into my revolutionary Black female self. I was enlightened by my Black feminist group, but the journey continued beyond those meetings. I found radical kinship via online groups, community organizing, and the power of music, specifically, *A Seat at the Table*. Black women are at the core of the album's messaging, and Black women showed up and showed out for Solange, sharing the album with our friends, playing it at events, and using the album to alter the way we approach activism, to create spaces in the world for ourselves.

While I was writing *Why Solange Matters*, I sent a call-out asking for anyone who was affected by Solange's work to get in touch.[4] I was inundated with messages from Black women. For Ally Hickson, a New York–based writer who diverged from her usual news beat to cover the album for *Refinery29* because it had such a profound impact on her, the album brought out a deeply emotional response. "I remember being home with my mom in Philadelphia at the time and riding the train into town and listening to the album, and I started crying. And my mom was like, 'Why are you crying?' And I was like, 'Oh, it's just so fucking good.' It's like everything I feel right now and everything I wish I could put into words, and she's done it not just with words, but with music too."[5] For Didi Jenning, the Washington, DC–based cohost of *Black Girl Squee!*, a podcast celebrating Black women, *A Seat at the Table* was an experience that couldn't be shared with everyone. "For the most part, I talk about this album with other Black women. I don't feel comfortable talking about it with people besides Black women. I don't know if anyone else would really understand."[6]

The communal nature of the album that Jenning mentioned is reflected in the way many people chose to listen to it. In April 2017, Janine Francois and Gabrielle Smith were so moved by the lyrics they organized the listening party "A Seat at the Table: Critical Reflections." The event was one of many Solange listening parties organized by various groups, and it welcomed a majority Black female audience to take in the experience together. Though the event welcomed everyone, organizers made it clear that the space was specifically for Black women, a caveat Francois was glad she added, as it "translated into the kind of room we established."[7] The small South London venue (Brixton's 198 Gallery) was packed with women who, after first entering the space with caution, unsure how to let go in typical British reserve, gave in to the atmosphere the album created, singing and dancing with one another as freely as they would in their own bedroom. I spoke to Jessica Ashman, a London-based animator, who attended the event and described the emotion in the room that night as having a "sense of freedom and fun, and again, this really interesting mix of political and artistry."[8] Smith described the event as unleashing a "liberating feeling" in her, adding that, like Ashman, she recognized the beauty of how the event impacted her community: "Sometimes if you're listening to it on your phone or on Spotify, you might be on your way to work or you might be at home, but you're not listening to it with people. It means something to you, but to come to a space where you're listening to it with other people, it might mean something different to them, and you can have that discussion about it."[9]

For many, it was the first time listening to the album in a majority Black space. For others, like Francois, it brought home the reality that they rarely were able to experience moments when they were not surrounded by whiteness: "It made me realize this is one of the few times I've been in a predominantly—outside of a family event—Black space and what does that mean in a city like London, where there are a number of Black people, but we don't have Black-specific spaces, and why, and what is that history. As someone who's interested in culture, what is my responsibility to create Black spaces, so that was really interesting. That was for us—'F.U.B.U.,' like that song—what is our responsibility to ensure the spaces of regeneration and rest and joy for Black people in a world that tries to do the complete opposite and take from us and abuse us."[10]

Francois's and Smith's efforts to bring women together around art made them rethink their approach to radical organizing. Similarly, in New York, the photographer and artist Seher Sikandar used art for healing. When Red Bull Music Academy commissioned Sikandar to create a project based on *A Seat at the Table*, Sikandar produced the lovingly compiled book *Testimonies from the Table*. The book featured images of Black female Solange fans and their descriptions of how they cope with the challenges of living in America. Competition to be involved in the project, which would later be hand delivered to Solange, was fierce. Sikandar whittled down the applications, choosing sixty-one women to make handwritten notes. She photographed them all in one day at her New York apartment. In the final book, one contributor, "Simone," thirty-six, wrote about her challenges, declaring that her "humanity is not a topic for debate."[11] It is Simone's response to the theme of healing that is most illuminating, and one that documents the power of female relationships: "When I walk into a room I carry my mother, my grandmothers, my ancestors and all of the women who have poured into me and created a way out of no way. I come from warrior women. My crown has been bought and paid for. I am free so I wear it proudly and pass it on. . . ."[12] Her portraits show her defiant and poised, resting her fist on her chin in one image, vibrant and smiling in another, with a small cartoon crown hovering above her.

Sikandar was moved by the show of camaraderie she created by simply bringing people together: "At one point, I think around 3 p.m. or 4 p.m. in the afternoon, there was the highest rush of the day, for whatever reason. I think people that had been sticking around and the new people that were coming in, and there were people on my couches, on the floor, everywhere. It was people, friends, that were girlfriends that didn't know their friend was gonna be there, or running into people they hadn't seen in years, or making new friends. There was a girl with headphones making her page and listening to music. It was such a beautiful energy. It was really, really powerful. It was like Black girl summer camp."[13]

For many Black women, the Black girl summer camp element of *A Seat at the Table* gave them an opportunity to reach out to other women, building on an already nourishing sense of community. Black women could use the album as an inside joke among themselves while in predominantly white workspaces or to celebrate the expansiveness of Black womanhood. Ultimately, what *A Seat at the Table* inspires in many Black women is a sense of joy; what we do with it is up to us. This was a reality Melissa Harris-Perry came to realize when she was asked to host an event on Black Girl Magic with Solange at Stanford University. Though she was a fan of the record, telling me she had probably listened to "Cranes in the Sky" a "thousand times a day for the first six months after the album dropped," she was unsure about taking the gig due to her busy schedule.[14] Then she saw her star mentee Mankaprr Conteh's reaction and realized she had become "a bit numb" to the importance of events like this: "I sit across the table from Anita Hill, or, you know, folks, and when I looked at this young woman who was my mentee [Conteh] and realized through her eyes how big this was and how much this meant to her as a young woman, that was part of the decision to say yes and to go."[15] Black women's admiration for *A Seat at the Table* has not gone unnoticed by Solange, who has spoken about how delighted she is to know Black women have taken the album to heart: "The biggest reward that I could ever get is seeing women, especially Black women, talk about what this album has done, the solace it has given them."[16]

DON'T TOUCH MY HAIR

My natural hair is a confusion. The soft wisps of fluff at my crown have no business sitting next to the tough, tightly wound curls that congregate near my temples. Neither patch seems to want anything to do with the fast-growing mass at the nape of my neck that constantly threatens to transform into a mullet if I don't trim it regularly. Don't get me wrong, I found joy in my hair ever since I first went relaxer-free in my early twenties. I became addicted to the light resistance my fingers found every time I ran my hand through my curls. I love my hair, but I'm also lazy, and by 2017, I needed an easier style for my "incapable of deep conditioning on a regular basis" self. I opted to get the "big chop," normally a process in which Black women transition to a natural style by cutting off chemically relaxed hair. I went to my hairdresser far more certain of my decision than my stylist, who asked me twice whether I was ready for this. I was ready, and so out came the clippers and off came my curls, leaving behind a short, cropped Afro.

As I stared in the mirror, I was certain I was as cute as I had ever looked, and walked out of the salon, almost skipping down the road with happiness. I imagine Solange had the same feeling when she went for the big chop in 2009. Instead of the joyful praise I received from my friends, Solange had to deal with the media, who couldn't understand why a woman would shave her head. The British newspaper *Daily Mail*, known for its celebrity gossip and conservative takes, immediately went with the low blow and questioned her mental health: "The long-suffering sister of singer Beyoncé has long resented the comparisons to the famous diva. She once playfully said she would 'go crazy like Britney' if people kept comparing her to her sister. And it seems she might finally have flipped as she hit the streets of Los Angeles in a new shorn hairstyle yesterday."[17] Other outlets were less offensive but no more impressed. MTV News wrote: "The motive is still unclear, but considering how gorgeous her mane was, it's not a great style choice."[18]

The reaction to what should have been a normal, unannounced haircut unfolded into an attack on a woman for stepping outside of the norms of femininity. It also showed white people's lack of knowledge about one of the most essential aspects of Black culture: our hair. Solange fired back in a series of tweets calling out those who made her the #3 trending topic on Twitter that day, above the Iran election:

> i. have. done. this. twice. in. my. life. i. was 16. i was 18. did. not care about your opinion. then. dont. care. now.
> i. just. wanted. to. be. free. from. the. bondage. that. Black. women sometimes. put. on. themselves. with. hair.[19]

The attention resulted in Solange becoming an unofficial figurehead of the then-nascent natural hair movement, and she found herself humbled by the women who proclaimed that she was their inspiration for embracing their curls. She appeared on *Oprah* and in Black publications like *Essence* magazine to talk about natural hair. She also became an ambassador for the hair care brand Carol's Daughter and its campaign for women transitioning from chemically relaxed hair to natural hair.

Solange's hair is part of most people's introduction to *A Seat at the Table*: the album cover. Solange stares defiantly at the camera, her body angled away. Her hair, still holding the transitional multicolored clips used to exaggerate her curls, falls in waves around her makeup-free face. We see only her face and shoulders, but she appears to be naked. The raw shot fulfills Solange's original intention of creating an image that "invited people to have an up-close and personal experience," but it was not the original shot she intended to get that day: "I wanted to nod to the *Mona Lisa* and the stateliness, the sternness that that image has. And I wanted to put these waves in my hair, and to really set the waves, you have to put these clips in. And when Neal, the hairstylist, put the clips in, I remember thinking, 'Woah, this is the transition, in the same way that I'm speaking about on "Cranes."' It was really important to capture that transition, to show the vulnerability and the imperfection of the transition—those clips signify just that, you know? Holding it down until you can get to the other side. I wanted to capture that."[20] It is a striking image, one that helped define this era of Black culture, laying bare the need to work through trauma and toward healing. It speaks to those in transitional periods of life, showing that vulnerability and imperfection can also be as stately as a Black Mona Lisa.

It comes as no surprise, then, that one of the central

songs on the album is about hair. "Don't Touch My Hair" opens on a pulsating kick-drum beat while scattered synth notes back up Solange's wispy vocals. As the song continues, a flurry of chords cascade down like raindrops, brightening the mood until a horn section swoops in to back up Solange and Sampha's confrontational refrain, "What you say to me?" The video featured a small selection of the creative ways Black people wear our hair, showing the world the beauty in beaded braids, mini Afros, and finger-wave styles alike.

Much like another natural hair anthem, India Arie's classic "I Am Not My Hair" (the 2005 neo-soul-indebted single that depicted the many stages in the natural hair journey), "Don't Touch My Hair" is quietly subversive, with none of the upfront ferocity of Solange's previous clap-back tweet. Instead, the calm delivery reveals a woman who has experienced enough to believe so deeply in the power of her words that she doesn't need to raise her voice above a whisper to make her thoughts known. She has spoken now so you *won't* touch her hair, her skin, her crown, you'll know your place. She details the work she put into her crowning glory:

> You know this hair is my shit
> Rolled the rod, I gave it time
> But this here is mine

She, like other Black people, spent hours of their life clenching their teeth to distract from the burning heat of the salon hood dryers and digging their nails into their thighs to get through the final minutes of the chemical relaxer treatment while it smoulders on your scalp. Some of the most inventive Black hairstyles have been ridiculed for being too "ghetto" or "ratchet." The Black community has endured the difficulties to be able to claim ownership of the hairstyles we hold dear.

The phrase "don't touch my hair" was in wide usage for years prior to Solange's take. It was the lead segment on Black talk shows where women would joke about the looming white hand that would reach out of nowhere to run their fingers through our scalps. It was the topic of TED talks on the radical nature of natural hair. It even became a video game (Hair Nah, created by the developer Momo Pixel) that prompted gamers to prevent various white characters from touching their mane. It is the universality of the term in Black culture that allows Solange to address her Black audience directly within the song:

> They don't understand what it means to me
> Where we chose to go
> Where we've been to know

In *Elle* magazine, the writer Morgan Jerkins welcomed this direct address: "This is not the kind of music that is supposed to be readily understood by everyone; every song is a figurative course in the midst of a thoughtful, sumptuous feast for certain guests."[21] By centering Blackness within this conversation, Solange is reminding her community of the many ways to live within the essence of oneself without following mainstream white culture.

In 2017, when Solange was featured in London's *Evening Standard* magazine, *ES*, the photoshoot featured many styles from Solange, including a towering halo of blond braids, delicately styled, reflecting the versatility of Black hair. When the magazine came out, Solange appeared on the cover, minus her halo. The magazine photoshopped out her braids, seemingly unaware that in her interview she described braiding as "an act of beauty, an act of convenience and an act of tradition," going so far as to say it is "its own art form."[22] The *Evening Standard* quickly issued an apology, claiming the image was altered for layout purposes. Solange already had her response lined up. Sharing the unaltered version of the image on Instagram, she posted the caption "dtmh," aka "don't touch my hair."[23]

CRANES IN THE SKY

During a 2008 writing session with the producer Raphael Saadiq, Solange tried to focus on the task at hand but found she couldn't stop her mind from wandering elsewhere. She was coping with the breakdown of her first marriage, contemplating life as a young single mother, and working through an identity crisis after previously basing her sense of self on who she was in her relationship. She was experiencing a lot of self-doubt.

Trying to keep her head in the game, Saadiq handed

her a CD filled with instrumentals he thought would work for her album. It took her over two months to listen to the CD, and though it was clear none of the tracks would fit into *Sol-Angel and the Hadley St. Dreams*, one track did stand out. The skeleton of "Cranes in the Sky" was already there; the melancholic strings rising to crescendo over a wavering bass line and meditative drum beat. Her reaction to the bare-bones track was strong. She went to her hotel room and wrote an early version of the lyrics and melody we know now. Solange initially wanted to add different chord changes, but Saadiq could not find the original track to edit from, which allowed the song to remain as a pensive lament, always running through the same handful of chords. Solange also wanted to channel the transcendence of the jazz musician and composer Alice Coltrane and weave in "some of those frequencies that really puncture you and give release."[24] Alice, wife of the legendary jazz saxophonist John Coltrane, was a musical prodigy from an early age, playing organ in her local church. She was a pianist in John's band until his death in 1967. While in mourning, Alice taught herself to play a harp, which John had purchased, but it arrived after his death. Her work as a composer, harpist, and jazz innovator merged with her growing spiritualism and need for peace following John's death. Her compositions cover North African music, Sanskrit chanting, jazz, New Age, and gospel, forming the foundations of her devotional music. It is in the calming repetitions of the looped drum beat and the blissful hum of the string section that Solange conjures Alice.

"Cranes in the Sky" is an achingly honest reflection on the loneliness experienced in the depths of depressive episodes, so much so that it is almost hard to hear Solange meditate on the many ways we cope with our mental health:

> I tried to drink it away
> I tried to put one in the air
> I tried to dance it away
> I tried to change it with my hair

Singing along, as the listener, we know where this will lead. Making these superficial changes won't make a difference in how she feels. The listener knows because who among us hasn't decided to switch things up to get over an ex-partner or stayed out all night in dank, sweaty venues hoping the closeness felt when pressed up against others will translate to emotional bonding. Often these distractions become cyclical and can be hard to break free from. Within the unconventional rhythmic structure and melody of "Cranes in the Sky" is an urge to slow down and reflect on the best and worst of your past. In this, it becomes possible to imagine discarding those coping mechanisms. The Grammy Award–winning song is one of the few occasions on the album where Solange's lyricism leans toward the metaphorical, perhaps referencing the struggle to put a direct name to fears.

It was her Miami writing stint with Saadiq that inspired

the references to cranes and metal clouds in the sky. Despite Miami's reputation as a party town, Solange had a deep love for the city, seeing it as a place of refuge. While she was in Miami, there was a real estate boom and the half-finished condos that littered the city transformed the skyline into an eyesore and altered her view of Miami as a place of calm and peace. She said of the moment: "I remember thinking of it as an analogy for my transition—this idea of building up, up, up that was going on in our country at the time, all of this excessive building, and not really dealing with what was in front of us. And we all know how that ended. That crashed and burned. It was a catastrophe. And that line came to me because it felt so indicative of what was going on in my life as well. And, eight years later, it's really interesting that now, here we are again, not seeing what's happening in our country, not wanting to put into perspective all of these ugly things that are staring us in the face."[25] Her reference to the 2008 housing crisis suggests that the song can also be read as a critique of the gentrified skylines that erupt out of many previously Black neighborhoods. Once shelters for the community, they are now home to overpriced cafés, vegan hotdog restaurants that only accept credit cards to keep out the working poor, and luxury apartments—all in the effort to lure more upper-middle-class people to the area.

She translated the inertia she felt while staring at the Miami skyline in the video for "Cranes in the Sky," using various pieces of wearable art to project the solemn mood of the track. Her most memorable piece is an oversized pink foam sweater she wore regally for much of the video. Solange originally contacted the Berlin-based designer Nadine Goepfert, requesting to wear the item at the Met Ball. After being turned down by Goepfert, who told her the piece was far too heavy to wear down the red carpet, Solange contacted her again a few months later asking to use the piece for her video. The sweater, designed for Goepfert's 2013 collection "The Garments May Vary," is made from around twelve pounds of memory foam mattress and is designed to force the wearer to "move differently."[26] Nadine talked to me about the meaning behind her design: "It's a very interesting material, because when you compress it, it will capture or stay compressed only for a few seconds, and then it will go back to its original state again, so you will not notice any compression afterwards. So, when I found this material, I felt like, yeah, that's interesting, because it captures movement and compression, but only for a few seconds."[27]

Seeing Solange burdened by this heavy yet soft piece of art that captures her memory and movement in a music video about coping with the weight of depression feels especially poetic. In the video, while she is wearing the foam sweater, she remains stationary, only able to make slight movements; a move of the head here, a rock from side to side there. She remains trapped by depression, despite appearing perfectly serene; both the garment and her mental health are a heavy load that she carries.

The video also sees Solange perform with a group of

Black women who bring out the communal themes of the album. From desert settings to a futuristic, cliff-top mansion, Solange lies with her girls, supporting one another from the weight of the world. In other scenes, she performs a series of slow, ritualistic moves she created to help reconnect with her body. Sometimes only Solange would perform them. In other scenes, she would be joined by another dancer performing the same moves. The mirrored dance moves showcase a way to break the cycle of poor mental health by letting others in on your state of mind. Let them perform your moves with you. Let them rest your head on their lap in silence. Let them listen to the words you wrote.

MAD

The angry Black woman myth has been rooted in popular culture for centuries. It is a weapon that has been used to paint Black women as villainous creatures and forced us to subdue our emotions. In reality, suppressing your emotions to create a passive environment for white people to live in is tiring work. After years of pushing it down, as a Black woman you start to realize: who am I without my emotions, what am I forgetting, and surely, as Solange insists, I "have a right to be mad," but how do we live with that anger? Much of the album was a journey toward better understanding "How can I exist with all of this rage and all of this pain and all of this anger? How can I possibly exist every day out here in the world with that? How do I turn that into glory? How do I turn that into power? How do I transcend with all of that facing me so closely?"[28]

Our fear of our own anger does not mean it should be avoided. Black women scholars have argued that Black female rage can be owned, accepted, and utilized in the fight for freedom. The author of *Eloquent Rage: A Black Feminist Discovers Her Superpower*, Brittney Cooper, spent years trying to mask her anger until a student in her class complimented her on her rage-filled lectures, appreciating the authenticity of her emotion. It was then that Cooper began to see her anger in a different light. Cooper told NPR, "We think about superpowers as, like, Batman using his smarts to outwit everybody or whatever. And I just think, you know, the biggest superheroes we've ever had, have been Black women who have looked at a set of conditions that are designed for them to fail and designed to kill them and said, we're going to live anyway. And not only are we going to live—we're going to thrive." She went on, "Part of what I'm trying to get at is that black women are never only angry. We can be angry and at the same time be joyous, at the same time be sad, at the same time be deeply in love or be heartbroken. So, rage for me becomes the ground zero for the reclamation of Black women's full emotional lives."[29] Cooper instructs Black women to reclaim their anger so as to remind themselves of their full humanity and that they deserve to express their emotions like anyone else.

"Mad" revels in the beauty of Black female rage, reminding us we are not overreacting. Though a fiery delivery would have been appropriate, too, Solange keeps her vocals floating in a falsetto range that her heroes singer-songwriter Joni Mitchell and soul singer Syreeta Wright would have been proud of, to drive home her point. Her delivery portrays a woman in control, one who has the upper hand and can express herself with ease:

> You got the light, count it all joy
> You got the right to be mad
> But when you carry it alone you find it only getting in
>   the way

Solange reminds Black women that when anger is kept inside like a secret, it can fester, impacting your mental health and well-being. The nagging voice of an unsympathetic other frequently asks why she can't just let it all go or why she has to be so mad. As a Black woman who deals with the low hum of microaggressions every day and has to defiantly love herself in a world that often refuses to reciprocate that love, Solange reminds the unsympathetic other that she most definitely can express herself in whatever way she feels like. "Mad" is not only a song about Black female rage, it also brings in a Black male perspective through rapper Lil Wayne's verse, where he delivers a gut-wrenchingly honest retelling of his own story of self-destruction. The section in which the rapper speaks on the burden of societal pressures, drug abuse, his suicide attempt, and other people's lack of understanding of his mental health brings to light the many pressures Black men also face when coping with anger.

The refrain of "Mad" puts forward the question "Where'd your love go?" It seems to be asking the listener to remember, as Cooper says, that softness can often ride alongside rage and that Black women deserve to go back to love. The iconic African American writer Maya Angelou understood that need for love, that if anger does not consume you, it can be a weapon. In an interview with the comedian Dave Chappelle in 2006, she said: "You should be angry. But you must not be bitter. Bitterness is like cancer. It eats upon the host. It doesn't do anything to the object of its displeasure. So, use that anger. You write it. You paint it. You dance it. You march it. You vote it. You do everything about it. You talk it. Never stop talking it."[30]

ON THE ELEVATOR

Anger and being visibly emotional has at times defined Solange's public persona far more often than she would care for. The most obvious example was her 2014 altercation with Jay-Z. Beyoncé, Jay-Z, Solange, and a bodyguard were caught on the Standard Hotel's elevator CCTV footage on May 5, 2014, after attending the Met Gala. The footage, leaked by a hotel security guard to TMZ, shows Solange lunging at Jay-Z, throwing kicks and punches wildly, while a bodyguard struggles to restrain her. Beyoncé looks on calmly, suggesting either that she wasn't surprised by her sister's outbursts or that Jay-Z committed something truly heinous to deserve the beating he received. The scandal was discussed for weeks, leading to inaccurate speculation about Solange's mental state. The family released a joint statement shortly after the leak stating, "The most important thing is that our family has worked through it," adding "Jay and Solange each assume their share of responsibility for what has occurred."[31]

As a notoriously secretive family, not one of the trio has ever publicly addressed the cause of the fight. The rumors that Solange was defending Beyoncé after finding out Jay-Z cheated seemed to be confirmed by the couple's next albums: *Lemonade* (2016) and *4:44* (2017), Jay-Z's response and lyrical acceptance of guilt. Some fans joke that three prodigious albums were conceived in that elevator. While the importance of each respective artist and the influence the moment had on their work cannot be denied, it came at the expense of Solange, who for years was the butt of jokes for her outburst.

At the time, Solange was well known in fashion and music circles, but she intentionally avoided her sister's spotlight, disliking the way celebrity obsession impacted her sister's life. The elevator incident threw Solange into the tabloid world she despised, opening up her private life to the masses ready to label her an "angry black woman." Even before this incident, the press enjoyed painting her as a brat, entitled, or stuck up. In other words, they saw her as uppity, a Black woman acting above her station. A Black woman who didn't cower at the sight of whiteness. A Black woman who knew herself and knew exactly how to speak her mind. If we are to believe Solange acted in defense of her sister, the fight, though violent, isn't all that unusual.

Solange is one of a long line of creative and unconventional women whose public outbursts, whether justified or not, have led to them being cast as unstable women. In 1996, Björk attacked a reporter at Don Mueang Airport in Bangkok when the woman tried to speak to her ten-year-old son. Paired with her history of eccentric behavior and her hatred of celebrity, which she described to the *Observer* in a 2007 interview as feeling like a "service job," the incident was the perfect excuse to brand the singer as crazy.[32] Another woman who has been demonized by the press is the Irish singer-songwriter Sinéad O'Connor. In 1992, at the end of her live performance on the NBC variety show *Saturday Night Live*, O'Connor tore up a picture of Pope John Paul II in protest against systemic incidents of child abuse in the Catholic Church. Though the history of physical and sexual abuse in the Catholic Church is well known now, in 1992, years before the horrors would become public, it was seen as an attention-seeking, unprovoked attack on a beloved institution. Her records were boycotted, and her profile in America took a major hit.

All three women fell victim to our society's outlandish reactions to unconventional women. They were all made an example of, to warn women that humiliation is in your future if you choose this path. Of course, as many women have discovered, losing the respect of those you don't respect may not be that bad in the long run. As they shriek and yell about the ways you've fallen out of favor with the ideal woman gods this time, you can look around, find the like-minded souls who will have your back, and get to work on creating a safe place for people like you.

LET'S TAKE IT OFF TONIGHT

Sometimes when my body gives up on me, and my mind refuses to stop running through the most embarrassing moments of my life, I take some time for myself. I bought adult coloring books and proceeded to use them once and immediately throw them away. When I managed to work up the energy, a productive session at the gym could pull me together. The most effective method I found to relax my brain came through gardening, or more specifically, trying not to kill the many houseplants I bring into my home. Taking time to water, repot, and sometimes merely stare at them, remembering that every seed starts out the same, gives me some sense of perspective. My performative self-care brought me respite for a short while, but long term I would eventually sink back into the uncomfortable anxiety that is within me.

At first, I thought I never gave it enough time, but slowly I came to realize the pressures Black women face weighed far too heavily on me for these small, superficial gestures of self-care to ever make much difference. Behind the strong Black woman façade imposed on us, we are coping with the effects of racial trauma, living below the poverty line, work discrimination, sexual abuse, emotional abuse, and a dearth of love in our lives—all while being expected to care for everyone else. These traumas impact our mental health. According to the UK government's 2017 Race Disparity Audit, in 2014, 29 percent of Black women said they recently experienced a common mental disorder compared to 21 percent of white women.[33] Similarly, in the United States, a 2015 study, led by Krim K. Lacey from the University of Michigan, found high rates of anxiety disorder (23.7 percent) in Black women, noting that severe physical intimate partner violence was associated with negative mental health conditions.[34]

Black women's awareness of our mental health struggles has made the practice of self-care an essential part of our lives. "Self-care" is a term that has been so overused it can describe nothing more than lighting a few candles and taking a bubble bath. If you Google "Black women and self-care," you will be greeted with an endless scroll of blogs and articles detailing how to perform self-care in the workplace, at home, or in a relationship. The practice has been hashtagged and memed to eternity with feel-good quotes from feminist authors routinely making the rounds on social media. Take it back to its radical feminist roots, though, and self-care is an inherently transgressive act, as it advocates for Black women to find value in themselves beyond what they can offer the society.

Self-care in this understanding is also about putting oneself in a better position to understand and dismantle the systems that have required us to need self-care in the first place. The credit for this practice is often given to the Black feminist scholar Audre Lorde, who famously said, "Caring for myself is not self-indulgence, it is self-preservation, and that is an act of political warfare."[35] Lorde's radical interpretation imagines Black women as warriors who need to rest mentally and physically if they want to win the war. As Jennifer C. Nash explains in her essay when analyzing the work of the American academic Patricia Hill Collins and her reading of Black self-love, "Love is a politics of claiming, embracing, and restoring the wounded black female self."[36]

The self-care methods of Nash and Lorde require Black women to love themselves enough to believe they deserve rest and put themselves first, a practice that can feel unfamiliar to many Black women who are used to shouldering the emotional burden of everyone around them. As the author of the book *Fat Girls Deserve Fairy Tales Too*, Evette Dionne said in a 2016 interview with *Bitch* magazine: "Many of us are poor, many of us are working ourselves into graves . . . so saying that I matter, that I come first, that what I need and what I want matters I think is a radical act because it goes against everything that we've been conditioned to believe."[37] And, as the Combahee River Collective, a Black feminist lesbian organization formed in 1974, said in its statement on why they organize, "We realize that the only people who care enough about us to work consistently for our liberation are us. Our politics evolve from a healthy love for ourselves, our sisters and our community which allows us to continue our struggle and work."[38]

Healing, by putting oneself first—as an individual or

as a people—is a theme that jumps out of *A Seat at the Table*, and it was influenced by Solange's need to find a new, daily form of self-care to tackle the anger she had been experiencing for years. She tried meditation but found she couldn't stay focused when left alone with her thoughts. Eventually, she discovered the benefits of repetition as a meditative force. Speaking to her friend Earl Sweatshirt on *Red Bull Radio*, she discussed how repetition, both in terms of her art, her dancing, and her approach to life, grounded her as a person. "Through repetition, if I just repeat a word, over and over and over again, then slowly I'll silence my mind."[39] She expanded on her repetition therapy to develop a meditative choreography, repeated over and over until each move became second nature, a dance embedded in her psyche.

The act of creating through repetition is one favored by the postmodernist choreographer and dancer Trisha Brown, whom Solange has acknowledged as a notable influence. The historical scholar Susan Rosenberg suggests that Brown, in her most well-known piece, 1983's *Set and Reset*, was "trying to rein in the esprit of improvisation in a fixed choreographic form."[40] To do this, she improvised movements that were remembered, recorded, and then perfected, creating moves that felt improvised in the moment. Solange's lean into improvisational choreography was developed over six months at the end of 2015 when she repeatedly tried out new versions of free-form movement, some of which she claims were a "hot mess," while recording herself on her iPhone.[41] These repeated movements incorporated her own mudras, symbolic hand gestures or poses associated with Indian spirituality that guide energy to different areas of the body. On her self-care practice, Solange has said: "I wanted to create the practice of really having, again, the space and the time to sit with myself and get to know my body better, and come up with a language of movement in a way that I was really leaving my body for once and letting my body lead."[42] The prominence given to her movements in her videos and live performances following the album release showcased this development. On stage, she would stand in a line with her backup singers performing slow, subtle movements. A drawn-out dip accentuated by jazz hands here, a whole body flop there—all precisely choreographed to mirror the energy of the music. In Brown's experimental processes, Solange has found a method to reconnect with her body and position herself within the modern dance movement.

Solange's journey of self-reflection and healing is documented in the hauntingly introspective "Don't Wish Me Well." Much of the backup track consists of the same looped, arpeggiated synth, reproducing her wider mantra for seeking grounding through repetition. In a calm, measured falsetto, Solange begins retelling her need to step back:

I went away
This concrete don't have love for me
I took a day

Too much talk and not much to see

Solange explains that she removed herself from the world she was in, suggesting that there was "not much to see" or that there wasn't a lot beyond the superficial she could connect with.

Her reference to concrete evokes the image of the packed concrete city streets Black women have to walk, traveling to workplaces where they are more often than not underpaid, undervalued, and placed under undue stress. In a *Guardian* article, the writer Anni Ferguson detailed her quest to find out more about Black women's mental health struggles, going so far as to create a WhatsApp group for Black women called "HELP!," where Black women shared struggles that often linked back to problems at work. Ferguson included twenty-seven-year-old teacher Michelle's response: "Why do I have to change who I am so that people don't find me intimidating or aggressive? It's tiring to have to always conform to get ahead."[43]

Morphing into a tamer version of yourself to put white people at ease, also known as code-switching, is an act of performance that has been utilized by practically every Black person at one point or another. No Black person remembers who taught them how to perform this act; it is hardwired in our brain as a mode of survival. But what if Black people chose not to cringe silently at Dave's racist joke at the watercooler or ignore Susan's curt tone? What would it look like for Black people to be able to be their full selves whenever they wanted? In the second verse, Solange puts this theory to the test and debuts her new centered self, to the annoyance of naysayers who point out her changed persona. They are unaware, as Solange points out, that the joke is on them for not being able to accept her as she is. Solange extends this life lesson to the listener in the song's refrain, imploring them not to languish in the dark forever. Solange reminds any other Black women who want to make the journey she has made that she will "leave the lights on," illuminating the way in case they want to join her later, leaving the mic on for them to tell their own story. It is in this welcoming refrain that I feel the energy of the trans-formative Black feminist group I came of age in. I can see these women around me, talking and laughing and helping one another work through our thoughts, like community therapy sessions. I hear much of *A Seat at the Table* in this same vein; leaning on Black women's loving way of inter-acting with one another to support those who need it. It is why Black women have reacted so viscerally to this album and its inclusion of their struggles.

— 7 —

FOR US, BY US

In the summer of 2013, Black activists across the world worked passionately on local projects, sharing their work and thoughts online. Intersectionality (American scholar Kimberlé Crenshaw's theory that gives a name to how interlocking systems of power impact marginalized people) was constantly trending. It was beloved by progressive activists, who idolized the theory for its all-encompassing approach, but derided by white middle-class feminists, who saw it as a version of oppression Olympics. The fight for dignity and respect for Black people has seen a plethora of different leaders take the helm over the years, but there was as yet no single person or slogan that defined that era of Black activism. Then, in July 2013, George Zimmerman was acquitted of the murder of the Florida teenager Trayvon Martin. Stunned by the lack of justice, Alicia Garza wrote a Facebook post titled "A Love Note to Black People," in which she stated that "Our Lives Matter, Black Lives Matter."[1] Fellow activist Patrisse Cullors replied with a simple change to Garza's quote, summarizing the most important point and solidifying it into a statement, #Black-livesmatter. Opal Tometi added her support online, and the movement took off overnight. It was a seismic demonstration of the political power of social media and gave hope to Black people around the world.

Black Lives Matter. It was a concise slogan that cut to the heart of the brutal reality of how undervalued Black lives were just by the fact that the phrase was needed at all. Despite the discomfort some had with the saying (choosing to view it as divisive, instead using the clunky term All Lives Matter, or even worse, Blue Lives Matter to support the police), Black Lives Matter became a global talking point. The slogan also allowed parts of the Black community to express their intersectional oppression: Black queer, trans, incarcerated, Muslim, differently abled, immigrant, and undocumented lives matter, too. The movement imbued in those who uttered its words a desire to protect Black communities at all costs and a renewed awareness of the benefits of on-the-ground activism. Like many others, Solange found herself caught up in the movement. On July 14, 2013, Solange linked up with the Brooklyn NAACP and Brooklyn Youth Council to hold a rally at Borough Hall in Brooklyn to protest the Zimmerman verdict. Hundreds gathered on the historic building's steps, carrying placards, boomboxes, and speaker systems. Solange protested with a placard quoting Malcolm X's words, "I'm for truth, no matter who tells it. I'm for justice, no matter who it's for or against." The rally made its impact on attendees, who used the hashtag #BKLYN4Trayvon to alert followers to the event. Volunteer Christina Coleman tweeted her appreciation of Solange's presence: "I got a chance to lend a hand to the #BKLYN4Trayvon rally. @Solangeknowles Thank you for reminding our bros & sisters that we have voices."[2] Solange went home as revitalized as everyone else, saying later on Twitter: "Seeing & gathering with people today/tonight all for the same fight helped to restore my faith in humanity. Thank you to everyone who came out to support #Bklyn4trayvon rally! This was just a start to a long journey of Justice and Equality!"[3]

That same summer she began her first run of sessions for *A Seat at the Table*. The album's lengthy gestation allowed Solange to reflect on the changes she was witnessing in society. It inspired her and gave her perspective on other atrocities, like the death in police custody of Sandra Bland in 2015, and the police shooting of Philando Castile in 2016 and twelve-year-old Tamir Rice in 2014: "When I felt afraid or when I felt like this record would be so different from my last, I would see or hear another story of a young Black person in America having their life taken away from them, having their freedom taken away. That would fuel me to go back and revisit and sometimes rewrite some of these songs to go a little further and not be afraid to have the conversation."[4] Her dedication made *A Seat at the Table* a significant part of the conversation on Black activism.

THE STREETS SAY YOU'RE A KING

In 2015, at an HBO-sponsored event for the network's biopic of the legendary blues singer Bessie Smith, Solange introduced an early version of "Rise." She remarked that the song was written "for Ferguson, for Baltimore," referencing the civil unrest in both cities when Michael Brown and Freddie Gray, two unarmed Black men, died at the hands of the police.[5] Fast-forward a year, and the first notes of *A Seat at the Table* listeners hear come from "Rise," a mournful lament on state-sanctioned violence. Its placement as the opener denotes the importance of its message. Solange has referred to "Rise" as a "cleanser," preparing the listener for the journey the album will take them on.[6] The repetitive lyrics and palliative tone in Solange's vocals give the song a mantra-like quality, lulling the listener into a contemplative state of mind. "Rise" is based around the vocal acrobatics of Solange. She layers her voice with contrasting harmonies, which, when combined, take on the shape of a celestial choir swirling around in the listener's head. Over the sparse, stilted beat, Solange offers directions to the listener, and perhaps to herself also:

Fall in your ways, so you can crumble
Fall in your ways, so you can sleep at night
Fall in your ways, so you can wake up and rise

Solange gives you permission to "fall" into yourself, to recognize the journey you and your ancestors took to reach this moment, and to be at peace with who you have been, in order to transcend into who you could be. Though the words "fall" and "crumble" suggest a state of emotional distress, as the song develops, the invitation changes to "walk in your ways," signaling a disruption in energy. The listener, now in this stage of the semiguided meditation, is equipped with the emotional stability to take in all that *A Seat at the Table* offers. Considering the array of themes the album contains, "Rise" can also be read as a mantra for the Black community to prepare for whatever fight we have to face in our everyday lives. Whether it is actively rebelling against a workplace that undervalues you or a political system that exploits you, recognizing the wrongs that have been committed against us is an essential step in naming our aggressor.

If "Rise" opens the album asking listeners to journey back through their past memories, the final song on the album, "Scales," could be a snapshot of one of those found memories from the life of a young Black man in America. Much like "Rise," the skeleton of "Scales" is rooted in a downtempo beat and a sparse piano melody. The song reads like a short story, written about someone that could be, or was, part of any African American household. The listener learns he likes his cars, his grill is always on, and he uses incense to cover up the smell, we assume, of weed. We learn about the dynamics of this family also:

And your mother is a queen
But damn she always tells ya

"You gon' end up like your daddy"
But damn that nigga fresh

In these lines, we can picture his mother, caring but strict. He treats her like royalty, and she expects it. His father is mentioned as the worst possible path he could take. He agrees with her, but deep down he still respects the life his father lived, despite the dark places it took him to. Solange tells us this man watches the TV and recognizes that the same oppressive society that kills Black people also tries to copy the community's style and swagger. He is aware of the political and cultural traditions that dictate the world he lives in and the hypocrisy of those who instill them. The direct nature of her lyrics resembles the everyday conversations Black people might have with a close friend, peppering the conversation with references to an indiscretion we came across.

These vignettes from this unnamed Black man's life are relatable and humanizing. With each shocking revelation that another unarmed Black person has been killed by the police, there always follows a frenzy to slander the character of the deceased. Mug shots, descriptions of suspicious clothing, or repeated insistences that they didn't comply are handed out in an attempt to justify the person's death. To reclaim their humanity and celebrate the complexity of Black life, "Scales" tells the story of those lost lives and those who are still being dehumanized today. It tells the story of Black men and women whose intelligence is overlooked, whose style is seen as suspicious, and whose strength is viewed as a threat as soon as they step outside their door.

F.U.B.U.

For years in my twenties, every Tuesday night after work I would travel to Old Street (an area of East London), pick up something delicious to snack on and share, and attend a local women's choir group. We sang everything from Scottish cattle calls to Hawaiian folk songs, all with the intention to bring protest music out of the songbooks and back onto the streets. Our choir leader, Shilpa Shah, would remind us, when we were burned out from anger, that music can revitalize our energies. London's Notting Hill Carnival founder Claudia Jones shared a similar belief in the arts. When the Carnival was first held in 1959, it was televised on the BBC, with the subtitle, "A people's art is the genesis of their freedom."[7]

It is through this lens that we can analyze Solange's dedication to performing her activism through her art. She has referred to *A Seat at the Table* as "protest music."[8] The apex of this musical resistance to the status quo can be found in the track "F.U.B.U." (aka "For Us, By Us"), a song that solely directs its attention to Black people. The title is a reference to the Black-owned streetwear brand of the same name, founded in 1992. By the late '90s the brand held a steady grip on the casual sportswear market, and at its peak, sales topped $350 million. FUBU's must-have appeal was captured in the second season of Donald Glover's HBO series *Atlanta*. In a nostalgic flashback episode, the lead character, Earn, wears a FUBU jersey to school on the same day as his classmate, which leads to a humiliating inquiry into which is the fake. Growing up in the '90s, Solange witnessed the same brand ubiquity as Glover (citing LL Cool J's controversial co-option of his Gap commercial by wearing a FUBU hat, a move that was beneficial for both brands) and felt empowered by the normalization of wearing a symbol of Black ownership: "'F.U.B.U.' exhibited Blackness in any space, on a huge global level, and that is what I wanted to do with the song."[9] The themes of Black ownership can also be heard on Master P's preceding interlude, where he retells the story of his brother's astonishment that he would turn down a million-dollar record deal so he could own his work and build a record label. "I said 'No, what you think I'm worth? If this white man offer me a million dollars I gotta be worth forty, or fifty. . . . Or ten or something.'" P continues, explaining how it wasn't only the opportunity to make more money that drove his decision to become an entrepreneur, "Being able to make 'Forbes' and come from the Projects. You know, 'Top 40 Under 40.' Which they said couldn't be done. Had twenty records on the top 'Billboard' at one time. For an independent company. Black-owned company."

Master P's story is one of self-belief in both his place in the music industry and his savvy entrepreneurship. His efforts were creatively and financially rewarding and gave him his place in the industry. His work also created greater visibility for Black-owned businesses, giving Black music industry figures another model to follow. Solange seems to be using FUBU and Master P as a vision of Black empowerment, replicating the pro-Black politics she found so inspiring as a child, but there are some flaws with her examples. What FUBU and Master P exhibit is a type of Black capitalism that has enriched their own lives but, beyond pure visibility, has not and will not liberate the Black community. Often when trying to promote ways to help the Black community, well-intentioned (and sometimes not very well-intentioned and only money-minded) people look to transformative Black ownership. In a world where capitalism rules, being able to physically see or touch something that is yours, or buy a product from within the Black community, can make Black people feel more secure. In reality, capitalism is a disease that relies on the existence of an underclass to thrive. Engaging in capitalism only demonstrates that Black people can play the white man's game to benefit a tiny percentage of the Black community. Replacing the white CEO of a billion-dollar company selling an overpriced product to the Black community with a Black CEO does not mean the Black community is no longer being taken advantage of; the oppressor merely has a new face. As the writer Aaron Ross Coleman said in his critique of Black capitalism in *The Nation*, "Black business offers mere Band-Aids to cover the gun wound of racial inequality."[10]

Though the supposed entrepreneurial liberation of

FUBU and Master P may not result in lasting radical action, the rest of the song "F.U.B.U." is still a significant, disruptive anthem for the Black struggle. Every part of "F.U.B.U." feels inherently black, even the slow march of the beat at the core of the track, which feels so deliciously dramatic it could be the backbone of a musical where Solange snaps her fingers in time, top hat and cane in hand, as she sings to her people a story of their history. If her message was not clear enough, Solange opens the song with the line:

All my niggas in the whole wide world
. . .
Made this song to make it all y'all's turn
. . .
Play this song and sing it on your terms

The direct nature of her delivery immediately signals who the song is for and who can sing along: Black people. Anyone who has been at a party with white people who are on the wrong side of tipsy when a song like Kanye West's 2005 hit "Gold Digger" comes on knows white people often don't take the hint that some words aren't for them. Nevertheless, "F.U.B.U." does attempt to put across the point many Black people in hip-hop have been reiterating for years when asked why they use the word "nigga," which is that *we* are not addressing *you*. The central narrative of "F.U.B.U." lays out the many everyday scenarios Black people find themselves in, which, in the blink of an eye, can be soured by the sting of racism:

> When it's going on a thousand years
> And you pulling up to your crib
> And they ask you where you live again
> But you running out of damns to give

Those lyrics were inspired by an incident in Solange's life. As documented in her essay "And Do You Belong? I Do," an officer refused to let her into her own neighborhood despite possessing a resident's pass. The fear and humiliation Solange felt at that moment was reflected in the original working title for "F.U.B.U.": "Be Very Afraid." Like a photo negative version of "F.U.B.U.," the song originally chose pessimism over optimism, conjuring the collective fear white people have of the Black community and the trauma of police violence. Tackling the numerous murders that hit the headlines in a four-minute song proved too painful. On the fifth or sixth variation of the song, something came over her, and she rewrote "F.U.B.U." in six minutes, creating the version we know now. In its current form, "F.U.B.U." takes back power from whiteness as Solange noted in an NPR interview: "There's a certain tonality of that song that also speaks to—when you exist as an unafraid and powerful Black presence in this country, what happens as a result of that?"[11]

The original title of "Be Very Afraid" positions fear on

both sides of the dynamic, perhaps because fear is the emotion that lingers in the air after experiencing racial violence or microaggressions. Although fear is a part of the Black experience of racism, to boil down our every feeling that arises in those moments to only fear centers whiteness in our narrative and positions Black people in a state of perpetual victimhood, constantly running away from or into the jaws of death. Black lives are far more complex than this. We feel the tension, the embarrassment, the ridicule, the predictability, and the mundanity of it all. By focusing on the dull reality of racism, Solange creates a collective experience that embraces everyone in the Black community in a self-deprecating depiction of Black life, reminding us that their fear will never break our spirit or rule our lives.

The choice to spotlight the macabre within the mundane was inspired by the award-winning essayist Claudia Rankine's 2014 book, *Citizen: An American Lyric*. The book details the microaggressions Rankine experiences in her daily life, the racist attacks against the tennis star Serena Williams, and the lack of care for Black lives. After an incident in Marfa, Texas, when the police came to Solange and her husband's Airbnb unannounced, a friend at a local bookstore recommended Rankine's book to Solange. She was instantly taken with the book, amazed that Rankine was able to succinctly express the emotions Solange also experienced. Speaking to *Fader* in 2016, Solange said:

"I think that, in the past, I might have been a bit more reluctant in my songwriting to be so clear in the narrative—I use a lot of analogies, and I try to have a certain sense of poetry in my writing—but I feel like [Rankine] really helped inspire me to be more direct in my feelings."[12] This directness allowed Solange to connect so deeply with her community, spouting takes like she was chatting with them under the hair-dryer hood of her mother's salon. The honesty in the lyrics plays out in the creative digital booklet that accompanies the album. In the pages for "F.U.B.U.," the phrase repeated the most in the song, "all my niggas in the whole wide world," is scattered across the page, each letter resembling individual pieces of a jigsaw puzzle that have been thrown across the floor. By turning the phrase into a jumbled anagram, Solange is reiterating the fact that the song is not meant to be deciphered by everyone.

In the same booklet, in the section for "Mad," there is a list of dates accompanied simply by the word "explaining." They run from 1619 and 1808 all the way to 2018. Two dates are highlighted with asterisks, 1965 and 1968, which denote two groundbreaking moments in the US civil rights movement: the Selma to Montgomery marches in 1965 and the passing of the Civil Rights Act of 1968. The text shows that Black people have been explaining their humanity for centuries, even after they supposedly no longer had to explain. It evokes James Baldwin's response to the opinion that Black people should wait for progress. As he succinctly expressed in the 1989 documentary *The Price of a Ticket*: "What is it you want me to reconcile myself to? I was born here almost sixty years ago. I'm not going to live another sixty years. You always told me it takes time. It's taken my father's time, my mother's time, my uncle's time, my brother's and my sister's time, my nieces' and my nephews' time. How much time do you want for *your* progress?"[13]

KNOWING WHEN TO LET GO

It seemed to happen gradually. First a post on social media, then one by one, more people dropped out of organizing meetings, until virtually no one was left. Around 2017, many of the community organizers I worked alongside or knew, whether it was in the punk scene or the political left, dropped out of the movement. Each one gave the same reason when announcing why they were stepping back: burnout. Coined in 1974 by the psychologist Herbert J. Freudenberger, "burnout" is defined as a "state of mental and physical exhaustion caused by one's professional life."[14] Activism by nature is a stressful endeavor, usually taken on by volunteers outside of their paid jobs because they feel a moral obligation to attend to the needs of their community. The fatigue of fighting the same fight over and over again, and the trauma uncovered when working on issues such as racism or sexual violence, makes burnout practically inevitable.

The activist and founder of the Equity Literacy Institute Paul Gorski wrote a 2015 paper in which he and his coauthor spoke to hundreds of activists and found that roughly half the activists who reported experiencing burnout left their movement for good. Speaking to *Vice* magazine in 2018, Gorski said: "When you have so many people burning out and leaving, it really messes up the potential for these movements to be effective. You're always mentoring new people, there's no consistency in who's engaged, and everyone's exhausted all of the time and snapping at each other."[15] This pattern played out in the London activist and DIY punk movements I was involved with. Tired of the pressures of trying to make a community in the increasingly expensive city, many activists up and left, moving to smaller cities across the UK. Few took up the same roles they once had in London within their new communities.

If we want to promote the healthy growth of activist movements that support the individuals at the heart, self-care is a necessity. This is the theory Solange works through on "Borderline (An Ode to Self Care)," composed to manifest the process of self-care more in her own life. "Borderline" embodies the slow-moving funk of mid-90s soul, brought to life by a dominant snare beat that forces the listener to sway along. The nostalgia within the rhythms is driven by the track's interpretations of Aaliyah's 2001 posthumous hit "More Than a Woman." The subtle translation of a well-known track along with Solange's softly sung vocals creates a sense of ease in the listener, a song you can play when taking that well-needed "intermission" Solange speaks of:

We've been lovers on a mission (all the way)
But what's love without a mission

Wrapped up in the day-to-day tasks of distributing fly-ers in local areas, calling elected representatives, and pick-eting, it is easy to lose sight of the end goal. Even those not directly involved in the fight now have the frontline brought to them in the form of graphic videos of police bru-tality. While many believe they have to watch these videos to be aware of what is happening, the impact of constantly viewing violence can be traumatizing. In this respect, turn-ing off those videos can be a form of self-care, which Sol-ange herself has had to practice, as she mentioned to *W* magazine in 2016: "Just for the sake of being able to exist in that day, to exist without rage, and exist without heart-break. To be able to get up and tell my child to have a won-derful day and know that he'll be protected and nurtured and loved and treated like an equal contributor to society, I sometimes have to choose to not look."[16] In doing this, Sol-ange is taking a moment to step back from the "borderline" she speaks of in the song to find solace in her home so she can find love with her family and let go of the intense pres-sures that come with existing in activist spaces or watching graphic videos of police brutality. She tells an unidentified other, perhaps the listener, she knows they are tired, iden-tifying the martyrdom and difficulty of asking for help. She reminds them that we all need to take a break to remember what we are all fighting for.

WHERE DO WE GO FROM HERE?

If we are to view *A Seat at the Table* as a reflection of a period in Black protest music, what will the Black community take from this album and what will they leave behind? I went to the Black women I interviewed for this project to find out if *A Seat at the Table* had an impact on their lives beyond music.

The politics and themes articulated on the album were not new to my interviewees, but hearing an artist like Solange reiterate them strengthened their beliefs, as Didi Jenning explained: "I think it's bolstered what I already know and believe. It makes me feel better about setting up certain boundaries in the workplace. There's certain things that I will and won't talk about, certain things I will not tolerate, things that I'll question as politely as I can without getting fired."[17] Jenning also revealed that the album empowered her to focus on lifting up the voices of other Black women in her creative endeavors: "It's been important to me, and now after this album, it's even more important. It's why I do a series of podcasts with different Black women hosts where we talk about different aspects of the culture, just to get different viewpoints out there, but definitely centered around Black women. I feel that our voices are important, and we have a lot to say."[18]

I also spoke to the drummer in the London-based pop punk band the Tuts, Beverly Ishmael, who was inspired to see the DIY outlook she connected with her punk scene endorsed by Solange. She just wished it were available a little earlier for her to take in as a teenager: "I feel like if I was fifteen, and listened to something like this, it would have changed my whole being." She continues, "It does encourage you to be more fierce . . . I feel like this album was like a DIY experiment. I don't think a label would've thought, 'Oh my god, yeah, you need to go down this road.'"[19] For Jessica Ashman, the album coincided with a heightened awareness of police brutality in the UK and the United States. She applied this political outlook to other areas of her life and found ways to talk about it: "I think maybe one of the most important things about Solange, and seeing her rise in that album, is that it made me feel a little bit of agency in the kind of things I can talk about in terms of where I sit as a Black woman (and as a mixed-race Black woman), how racism has affected my life, how it affects me now, and feeling like I can talk about that within my creative work."[20]

When I sit back and think how *A Seat at the Table* has impacted my approach to social justice, it is hard to isolate any one thing. For friends and me, the album became part of a conversation we were already having and gave us a context in which to unravel those ideas further. The album has also given me space for moments of reflection on the antiracist movement and my role within it. With my headphones on, taking in all that *A Seat at the Table* has to offer, I am emboldened remembering the battles won and lost by previous generations; the insidious moments of prejudice that provoke my rightful anger; and the dazzling, daring, and visionary Black community I seek to protect.

— 8 —

WHEN I GET HOME

Days before the US presidential election in November 2016, Solange was the musical guest on the long-running sketch comedy show *Saturday Night Live*. Backstage, she drank tea and sat with her family, preparing for her first televised performance since *A Seat at the Table* was released a few months prior. In a short video Tina Lawson later shared to Instagram, she and Beyoncé show their support by literally picking up Solange in their arms, despite her protests. Tina added a caption: "She's still our baby [heart emoji]. We have been picking her up like this since she was ten yrs old. On the legendary *SNL* stage [heart emoji]."[1]

Despite her family's encouragement, Solange was nervous. As she took the stage, which has also hosted her sister and brother-in-law, she at first appeared confident. She looked out over the audience, wearing an intricately constructed hair crown (designed by Chicago-based artist Shani Crowe and adorned with over two thousand Swarovski crystals) and a beaded silver dress. Defiant opulence in action. As she began to sing, however, her nerves asserted themselves on live television. Her voice was strained, unable to reach the higher register that made the sombre lilt of "Cranes in the Sky" so emotive. The lyrics, which she spent years perfecting, flopped out of her mouth in disarray. Throughout it all, she kept a plastered smile on her face, one that almost contorted into a grimace as the performance lumbered on.

The audience of the legendary comedy show is vast. Far bigger than the small but dedicated audiences she was used to performing for following *True*. The reality of who these words—written out of a need to exorcise inner demons from an explicitly Black female perspective—would reach hit Solange as soon as she stepped on stage. Aware that she was not performing these Black-centric songs in a Black space, Solange reflected that she felt "very naked" on stage at *SNL*.[2] That exposure culminated with a feeling of panic as she began to relive the traumas depicted in her songs. Singing "Cranes in the Sky" during this period was like "throwing salt on the wounds all over again."[3] During her first six performances in late 2016 and early 2017, her voice would quiver and shake. After the shows, she experienced intense panic attacks. The dissonance between the introspective soul-searching of the album's creation and the public consumption of her work for entertainment forced her to admit that the music she created as a sanctuary for healing was not as straightforward as she thought: "I'd love to say, 'Yes, I worked on the album, delivered it and it solved all of my problems and all of the complexities for me,' but it didn't. I'm trying to work through everything I felt on the album; it's a work in progress."[4]

Her performance problems were exacerbated by her health issues, which she was quietly coping with. She eventually announced in December 2017 that she had been treating an autonomic disorder for five months. It is a condition that affects the functioning of the heart, bladder, intestines, sweat glands, pupils, and blood vessels—all of which can limit the intense physical stamina needed to tour. In an attempt to reconnect with her body and work through her health problems, Solange focused even more on movement, making it a central part of her performances. Though she did not tour extensively, it is clear that when she did want to be in front of a crowd, she was determined to make it an experience rather than just a gig.

Like everything else, this was intentional. Solange strove to create a temple to the Black experience and took her show to festivals like Afropunk and Made in America, as well as majority-white spaces in institutions like the Guggenheim Museum and Chinati Foundation. Festival slots gave her a chance to split up her touring life so she did not have to spend months on the road. Performing in museum spaces made sense for Solange, who had aspirations to make art beyond the confines of the music world. In fact, she has become a modern-day Renaissance woman, creating conceptual performance art, making daring structural architecture installations, and collaborating with other artists.

These pieces allowed fans to view her music from a new angle or use her music as a bridge to explore other concepts. Some of these ventures were entirely removed from her life as a musician. Her work brought her into the prestigious halls of the Tate Modern in London. She plans to bring her visual style into homes around the world through Saint Heron's collaboration with the Swedish homeware company IKEA. The forthcoming GÅTFULL collection will feature products that aim to explore "time, space, light and matter."[5] Her conceptual approach to all of her work is inspired in part by the artist Sol LeWitt. In 1969, LeWitt wrote "Sentences on Conceptual Art," outlining his criteria for the form, much of which reflects Solange's practice:

> The concept of a work of art may involve the matter of the piece or the process in which it is made.
>
> Conceptual artists are mystics rather than rationalists. They leap to conclusions that logic cannot reach. Rational judgements repeat rational judgements. Irrational judgements lead to new experience.[6]

Much of her conceptual art practice—whether it be movement, music, or design—is born through improvised, repeated, and practiced processes that often emerge from her subconscious mind. This can be seen in the repeated movements she devises to calm her mind and choreograph new performances, or something as simple as jamming with her band until a melody makes its way out of the bustling noise.

Her work—not just her music—can also be described as minimalist with a penchant for the avant-garde, drawing heavily from artists like Donald Judd. Solange even performed her piece "Scales" with a troupe of musicians and dancers around fifteen sculptures by Donald Judd at the Chinati Foundation in Marfa, Texas. Her need to tackle a wide swath of art forms all at once could be seen as a form of artistic restlessness. The connection between her interior design collaboration with IKEA and her modernist performance art seems nonexistent at first. Each is a vehicle for Solange to showcase the art nerd in her while also finding new ways to evoke sensations that music alone cannot reach.

One of Solange's most successful efforts is the video and dance performance piece *Metatronia (Metatron's Cube)* (2018) at LA's Hammer Museum, which Solange directed, working closely with the choreographers Gerard and Kelly. In the footage, dancers dressed in all-black and all-white outfits move around a large white cube sculpture set to a score composed by Solange and John Carroll Kirby (who is also featured on both *A Seat at the Table* and *When I Get Home*). The movements of the dancers denote the positions on an analogue clock. Over time, these simple movements add a meditative quality to the dancers' rhythms, much like the sluggish but predictable back and forth of a metronome.

The sharp, minimalist, all-white M.C. Escher–esque cube at the center of her performance references sacred geometry, an ancient art that posits that universal patterns and sacred meanings are used in the geometric design of every part of our reality. The title is a reference to Archangel Metatron, an angel of life that oversees the energy flow in a cube, which contains every geometric shape in God's creation. Solange's take on the mysticism of sacred geometry brings a new spirit to conceptual art, one that is inherently Black.

Following in the footsteps of celebrated Black artists like Kara Walker, Betye Saar, and Adrian Piper, Solange has sought to challenge the majority white art world and put forward her own interpretation of the minimalist art movement. It is an interpretation that Erin Christovale, an assistant curator who oversaw the installation at the Hammer Museum, believes is intrinsically rebellious: "In a way she's challenging the legacy of this movement and who that movement belongs to because so much of that work is rooted in the creation of these very hard geometric shapes that are void of the figure, or nonrepresentational, and it brings up a really interesting conversation around what type of work can Black artists make, does it always have to be representational, and what happens when it's not, when it's totally abstract."[7]

Solange put that theory to the test at her 2017 performance at the Guggenheim Museum, where she brought her band and a troop of dancers to perform a piece titled

"An Ode To," a tribute to Black womanhood. Everyone in the Frank Lloyd Wright—designed rotunda adhered to the strict color theory dress code, the band in a selection of reds, browns, and yellows while the audience wore all white. In the cavernous room, which usually celebrated the work of white artists, the focus fell on this Black woman and her message that "inclusion is not enough," telling her audience they should all tear "the fucking walls down."[8] The performance in a prestigious venue allowed Solange to expand her visionary composition of *A Seat at the Table* and literally archive her work while performing.

As the performance ended, the strict choreography that kicked off the event dissipated and the band and Solange were overcome by the music. She threw herself to the floor, writhing around, flinging her head back and forth as if she had caught the spirit. It was a scene that stayed with many Black women there. Thelma Golden, director and chief curator of the Studio Museum in Harlem, was wholly inspired by the performance. "My life has been spent in museums. Waiting to go into the Guggenheim, I felt a range of feelings that remain hard to describe. What it meant to be in front of one of our great temples of culture. The space transformed, created, made into Black space, quite literally."[9]

By 2018, Solange could say that she now saw herself as a performance artist, adding, "I'm clear within myself that I'm not interested in entertainment at this moment."[10] In fact, it was her side hustles in the art world that gave her the breakthrough she needed for the next stage in her music. After receiving critiques that the high-art aesthetic of *A Seat at the Table* was "anti-Black" (based on the incorrect notion that art itself is a white medium), she asked her friends to hook her up with names of Black artists who created purely aesthetic work and refrained from using Blackness as their focal point. She was done, for now, with being the voice for a million of the world's weary. She wanted to live in the moment and create for the sake of creating. Recording *When I Get Home* in temporary studios set up in Airbnbs across LA, Houston, and Jamaica, she fell in love with making music again, jamming for hours with her collaborators. She was still touring *A Seat at the Table*, which created a cosmic link between the similar meditative energy embodied in both records. Now, her previous precise declarations of identity manifested themselves in a considerably more laid-back affair, in the form of *When I Get Home*.

MAKE YOUR TRUNK RATTLE

In 2018, *A Seat at the Table* still held the attention of the music world. Solange's status as a respected multidisciplinary, polymath artist for a generation led to her directing r&b singer SZA's video for her single "The Weekend"; becoming an official music consultant on actor and writer Issa Rae's hit HBO show *Insecure;* and earning countless accolades, including the 2018 Harvard Foundation Artist of the Year, a 2017 *Glamour* Woman of the Year, and the 2017 Billboard Impact Award. She was also honored for her iconic fashion at the 2018 70th Annual Parsons Benefit, in collaboration with the New School.

The critical and commercial success of *A Seat at the Table* catapulted Solange into a new league of revered artists, free to say and do as she pleased. She continued to lean into her arty persona, gracing the covers of cultural magazines such as *Surface* and *Cultured*. Her position within the industry was reflected in her choice to follow in the footsteps of other A-list stars such as Taylor Swift and Beyoncé, who often shy away from traditional journalist-penned profiles, opting instead to be interviewed by friends and contemporaries, or to write the story themselves. These pieces suggest an intimacy fans crave but reveal very little and allow celebrities greater control over their image. Solange's image control is partly due to her need for privacy (she has disappeared from social media numerous times and regularly deletes her posts), but it also reflects her wish to speak directly to those she sees as her audience, especially millennial Black music lovers.

Her wish to communicate directly with her fans was reflected in her next album rollout. On March 1, 2019, *When I Get Home* was released, symbolically drawing Black History Month to a close and kicking off Women's History Month. The short prerelease promotion showcased Solange's sense of humor, creating her own profile page on BlackPlanet, a 2000s-era social networking website for the Black community. A day before the release, she uploaded a series of Instagram clips, one of which included a caption with the phone number of the Houston rapper Mike Jones, who famously referred to the number in his songs and on his merchandise. When fans called, they were greeted by a recording of Solange, who informed callers that the album was going to drop that night. The nineteen-track album, and its accompanying film, was a clear evolution in sound and style for Solange, who brought together the ever-widening array of influences that inform her creative output. Deep funk ripples next to downtempo trap beats, while flashes of experimental jazz and '70s Afrofuturism merge with manipulated samples. The album is eclectic, but Solange's steady guidance as a coproducer and writer saves it from becoming chaotic. Though no song outstays its welcome—most clock in at under four minutes—the album does not feel rushed.

This technique is part of what makes *When I Get Home*, Solange's most "of the moment" album to date. The record follows the trend for avant-garde production in experimental r&b, where songs feel akin to a series of sketches that hint toward a particular mood. The mood in *When I Get Home* is ripped straight from the Black millennial handbook: music you can get high to, get your life to, and meditate to, often simultaneously. The scrapbook nature of the album's journey through spoken word, samples from classic records, and choice quotes from YouTube streaming sessions (the rappers Diamond and Princess from the Atlanta group Crime Mob and the spiritualist YouTuber Goddess Lulu Belle make brief appearances) demonstrates the fragmented nature of the way the millennial generation engages with culture. It is the soundtrack to many a lazy Sunday spent slumped next to a record player listening to the best of your parents' music collection while you scroll aimlessly through Twitter on your phone.

The extended-jam nature of the album is reflected in the composition of many of the songs. The laid-back chill of "Way to the Show" is captured in the delivery, which still possesses the repetitive mumble of the freestyle that birthed the song. Where *A Seat at the Table* quietly raged, *When I Get Home* looks ahead to a future in which the Black community can enjoy life at a slower pace. The record leaves the listener in an almost dreamlike state, immersed in the kaleidoscopic world Solange has created. I don't listen to *When I Get Home* expecting to have the same experiences and revelations as I have with *A Seat at the Table*. *When I Get Home* for me is about pure fun. It's for days when I want to dance alone in my bedroom and get lost in another world.

Compared to its predecessor, *When I Get Home* contains very few overtly political moments. "Almeda" is a celebration of Black culture, with its call for "brown liquor, brown skin" and "Black-owned things." Produced by frequent collaborators Pharrell Williams and John Carroll Kirby (also featuring stellar performances from rapper Playboy Carti and previous collaborator The-Dream), "Almeda" has a frenetic rattling beat that punctuates the importance of Solange's words. The song represents two separate but not completely dissimilar parts of the Black community. There is the late-night party vibe of the verses, as Solange extends her southern drawl to create a slurred effect on the lines "sip, sip, sip, sip." These sections remind me of the parties my friends and family have, where we can close the door to the outside world and live in the ground-shaking bass of the sound system. Alongside this, there is an almost sermon-like quality to Solange's preachings on Blackness, reminding listeners that "Black faith still can't be washed away / not even in that Florida Water." The cologne water is important to Solange and is used for spiritual cleansing rituals (she brought a bottle of Florida Water to the 2018 Met Gala and to her makeshift recording studio for the *When I Get Home* sessions). The line references the importance of traditional Black spirituality, as well as Black people's continual faith in themselves that cannot be diminished, no matter what is thrown at them. The contrasting party and faith themes in "Almeda" feel like the song should best be played in the waking hours of Sunday morning, when you need to come down from the club and get ready for praise at church.

Another Black pride anthem can be found in "My Skin My Logo," in which the Atlanta rapper Gucci Mane and Solange jokingly describe each other's swagger. As the pair swap stories of how they like to "go hard in the paint" and "drink" and "ball," the listener is given a peek into the creativity that composes African American culture. The clever wordplay and drawn-out vowels in both their styles make their lives sound increasingly endearing. As the song title denotes, their appreciation for their culture does not mean it should be up for grabs. "My Skin My Logo" is a demand for Black culture to be forever connected with Black people, and not appropriated out of context.

"My Skin My Logo" features choice moments from the rapper Tyler, the Creator and from Gucci Mane, a selection of the small army of collaborators who were part of the making of *When I Get Home*. Solange's voice and vision are so much stronger than they were on her debut that at times the listener is left searching for signs of her collaborators as their contributions begin to merge with Solange. Tyler, the Creator is barely recognizable on "Down with the Clique," and r&b singer Cassie's voice eerily morphs into Solange's on "Way to the Show." With its slick, washed-out funk, "Way to the Show" is evidence of Solange's desire to make a record that would "bang and make your trunk rattle."[11] Like much of the album, "Way to the Show" is moody and meditative in nature, with lyrics that spotlight the hometown she's trying to get back to:

Call me, even on the way to the show
Way to the show, candy paint down to the floor

The aforementioned "candy paint" is a reference to Houston's slab scene, where car lovers gather to admire one another's customized rides. Having the right rims, candy paint (a bright, translucent custom paint job), swangas (spoked wire rims that protrude from the car), and bass-rumbling stereo systems is essential. Once again, Solange is paying homage to aspects of her culture that are less known outside of her community. The instrumentals of "Way to the Show" feel almost nostalgic due to the squelching bass and exaggerated wah effect on the guitar riffs. A similar vibe can be heard on "Stay Flo," which is propelled by a steady bass line and ominous chord changes. The vocalizations that make up the chorus, paired with the sinister instrumentals, call back to a style of '90s hip-hop-backing vocals that would fit in nicely with the Oakland duo Luniz or the West Coast rapper Warren G. The nostalgic quality of the song and slowed-down two-step sway also make it a perfect candidate for the Electric Slide if ever the Black community needs a replacement for "Candy" by the '80s funk group Cameo.

The Caribbean-tinged "Binz" is sentimental for me, evoking memories of my childhood spent dancing in my grandma's kitchen to dancehall and soca. Over a simplified, 808-style beat, Solange freestyles about her perfect day waking up in Saint Laurent on "CP time." The latter is a reference to the phrase "colored people's time." A variation on this phrase is used across the Black diaspora and is a joke at the expense of Black people's supposed inability to get anywhere on time. In "Binz," it becomes an in-joke for the Black community. The track is ultimately tongue-in-cheek, as seen in the homemade-style music video, in which Solange jokes around with friends and twerks to the beat. She embodies the in-control sexiness of the '90s dancehall queen Patra, while bringing out the boastful qualities of the dancehall legend Sister Nancy. It is a moment that feels, like much of the album, inherently Black, but without trying.

These themes carry over to the album's accompanying film (directed and edited by Solange with contributing directors Alan Ferguson, Terence Nance, Jacolby Satterwhite, and Ray Tintori), which, it can be argued, is a studied look at Afrofuturism. The film brings together elements of performance art, dance, fashion, sculpture, and cinematography. Black men and women dressed in minimalist black attire with space-age metallic accessories stand proudly in a concrete-dominated city landscape, posed in scenes that look like the stylish aftermath of an all-Black revolution. Elsewhere, the female body in its many forms is celebrated, DIY spaceships are assembled, and gatherings within the middle of giant white sculptures take place. When paired with the appropriate visuals, the album takes on new life as a score to an avant-garde Black cinema.

When I Get Home also reflects her new love for overt sensuality. Solange wears skin-tight dresses, crystal negligées, and snakeskin boots, rocking a high-femme aesthetic rooted in the tongue-in-cheek style of stars like the influential rapper Lil' Kim. That style reflects an intrinsic campness in Black culture, showcased in the film through extravagant towering hairdos, black lip liner, and glimmering grills. The aesthetic plays on the way Black people use style as another form of expression, a theory documented by the African American anthropologist Zora Neale Hurston in her 1934 essay "Characteristics of Negro Expression": "Every phase of Negro life is highly dramatized. No matter how joyful or how sad the case, there is sufficient poise for drama. Everything is acted out."[12] Tapping into Black camp is one more way Solange strives to communicate directly with her audience.

The overwhelming theme of the film, though, is the Black cowboy aesthetic, another homage to Houston. Throughout *When I Get Home*, Black men and women in cowboy hats and thigh-high chaps grace the screen on horseback, riding in and out of shot, showing off their bull-riding skills and strolling on horseback through a Houston neighborhood. Solange knew she wanted to bring the cowboy aesthetic into the album from the start, going so far as to pin pictures of Black cowboys on the wall of her recording studios: "That was the moment to express this culture that was so enriching for me, and it's not just an aesthetic. This is something that we live on Sundays. I see so many of my friends who still every weekend are turning up at the zydeco [a blend of blues and r&b music indigenous to the Louisiana region]."[13]

The leather-clad direction came just in time for the burgeoning "yeehaw agenda," a term coined by Twitter user Bri Malandro at the end of 2018 to describe pop culture's renewed interest in Western imagery. The term went viral on Twitter when the writer Antwaun Sargent posted a photo thread demonstrating the artistry of Western-influenced attire. The thread included fashion editorial spreads, models, and celebrities including Beyoncé, Lil' Kim, and Mary J. Blige. The term has come to reference people of color placing themselves back into what Sargent has referred to as a "quintessential part of an American identity."[14] It was a revelation to many in the wider Black community who were unaware that Black people played such a crucial role in this essential chapter in US history. This knowledge helped Black people embody the majesty and freedom associated with the cowboy. They took the confidence of the straight white man, previously seen as the epitome of cowboy chic, and brought it into whatever area of life Black people needed most.

HOUSTON CALLING

You can hear it in the bounce of Solange's delivery, the stuttered compositions, and the world of southern references the record lives in; among many other things, *When I Get Home* is foremost an ode to Houston. Her nomadic life of touring and moving from city to city started when she was a teenager on the road with Destiny's Child. It was a lifestyle that left her constantly longing for home. This longing inspired what could be a rose-tinted reflection of her hometown. Solange does not dwell on any negatives of Houston, instead focusing on what she sees as the swagger that makes the city special and, in turn, made her who she is. She sought to capture the effect places that were part of her childhood had on her, like her memories of her mother's hair salon or of visiting the vast discount store King's Flea Market.

And so, her beloved Houston is brought to life, frozen in sonic time as late-night drives across the city (S. McGregor, Almeda, Exit Scott, Binz, and Beltway are all roads in Houston) on the way to meet your crew outside a club. Locals Phylicia Rashad and Debbie Allen serenade on a sample taken from a 1987 Mother's Day TV special *Superstars and Their Moms* while a distorted vocal utters "Houston, Texas" underneath. The interlude feels like a re-creation of Solange channel-hopping as a kid where she stumbled on a rerun of this clip. Elsewhere, the Houston-born Black lesbian feminist poet Pat Parker makes an appearance on "Exit Scott (Interlude)" as a distorted excerpt of her exploration of the romantic love for women, "Poem to Ann #2," rumbles in the background.

Houston's influential hip-hop scene was a clear inspiration for Solange. The local rapper Devin the Dude takes us out of "Dreams," a song about manifesting childhood fantasies, with a drowsy, whispered delivery, keeping in line with the hazy feeling one gets when reflecting on the past. Scarface (formerly a member of Houston's own Geto Boys) performs a stream-of-consciousness freestyle on "Not Screwed," which, thanks to Brooklyn's experimental hip-hop group Standing on the Corner, is treated to the pitch-warping production skills popularized by the

Houston producer, and key influence on this record, DJ Screw. The DJ and producer (who died of a heart attack complicated by codeine use in 2000 at twenty-nine years old) was known for the chopped and screwed technique, which incorporated pitched-down vocals, slower tempos, and unusual cuts to create a psychedelic, ethereal sound. The drowsy sensation you get when listening to Screw's music feels psychedelic for a reason, as Screw composed with a presumption that the listener will be high. "When you smoking weed listening to music, you can't bob your head to nothing fast."[15] As well as "Not Screwed," we also see signs of DJ Screw's influence on *When I Get Home* in the frenzied samples on "Can I Hold the Mic" and on the record's smooth transition from song to song. These transitions, interruptions from random samples or vocals, and the ability to pair wide-ranging genres like jazz with funk and hip-hop, make the album feel like one long DJ set, one that Screw might have bobbed his head to.

Growing up in Houston, Solange was introduced to the work of DJ Screw and other local acts like the southern gangsta rappers the Geto Boys. Solange spent her childhood taking in the city's thriving, if isolated, rap scene and remembers doing her homework to the soundtrack of independent Houston hip-hop label Swishahouse's *Fuck Action* tape. It was a scene that stayed with her: "I swear that pace and frequency has impacted the entire wavelength I operate from! I'm like, 'everybody need to slow the fuck down!'"[16]

When DJ Screw's Screwed Up movement was taking over the city, passed around on mixtapes, young kids like her were listening in. Lance Scott Walker, the author of *Houston Rap Tapes: An Oral History of Bayou City Hip-Hop*, explains what made Houston unique: "Houston's hip-hop scene in the 1990s and early 2000s when Solange was growing up there was different from the rest of the country because it was a largely independent scene. Geto Boys put Houston on the map when they switched to a major label, but the foundation of their whole career was through the independent Rap-A-Lot label."[17]

Solange looked up to self-made men like her father, so it's not surprising that she was drawn to the city's home-grown rappers like the Geto Boys. The devoted support DIY labels like Rap-A-Lot received in Houston in the 1990s and early 2000s reflects the camaraderie of the community and, as Walker tells me, the sheer scarcity of music available from other cities: "When [music] was less available, you heard more of it from Houston because there's just so much music in Houston, so many artists, that it floods into what a lot of people have been listening to over the years. Houston has legitimate superstars within the city who can make all of their money right at home, so even though Houston radio has been notoriously under support-ive of local music, the fans have made it to where those art-ists have been able to make careers for themselves and stay relevant in their own city."[18] The regionality of *When I Get Home* will earn the record a forever home in the hearts of

Houstonites all over, but it does not make the album inaccessible to outsiders. Listeners from around the world can appreciate Solange letting them in on the quirks that make her hometown what it is. Even if people do not know or relate to Houston, Texas, everyone has a home, a place they want to get back to, just as Solange did.

THE BLACK AVANT-GARDE

Solange has stated that *When I Get Home* came to life through a number of varied influences, including the minimalist composer Steve Reich, Joni Mitchell's jazz era, Minnie Riperton's classic album *Come to My Garden*, director Busby Berkeley's high-drama 1930s musicals, the Afrofuturist jazz explorations of artists like Alice Coltrane and Sun-Ra, the psychedelic soul band Rotary Connection, and Stevie Wonder's 1979 album *Journey Through the Secret Life of Plants*. In an effort to bring together the sounds she heard in her head, Solange referred to the work of her longtime producing heroines Björk and the hip-hop legend Missy Elliott, who were known for their avant-garde approach to music.

Much like Björk's, Missy Elliott's seismic impact on the music industry stretched beyond any one genre; artists from Blondie frontwoman Debbie Harry to Lil Wayne have sung her praises. Born in Virginia in 1971, Missy formed the all-female group Sista in 1991, recruiting childhood friend Timothy Mosley, aka Timbaland, to work on production. It was the beginning of a long and fruitful working partnership in which the pair wrote and produced tracks for r&b groups like SWV, 702, and most notably Aaliyah, whose second album, 1996's *One in a Million*, featured nine tracks from the duo.

Missy's debut solo release in 1997, *Supa Dupa Fly*, set the tone for her work: staccato rhythms; inconsistent and extended breakbeats; warped vocal samples; and Missy's catchy lyrics, which, whether sung or rapped, focused on the pleasures she wanted in life. The twinkling synthesizer refrain, choppy woodblock beat, and spacious composition of *When I Get Home*'s "Sound of Rain" are very Missy. Missy's earlier work focused on the love lives, breakups, and needs of her generation, often delivered in the nonchalant tone of songs like "The Rain (Supa Dupa Fly)." Her lyrical style was occasionally dismissed as lazy, but those critics failed to understand that Missy was using AAVE to speak to her own community. The narrative of "Sound of Rain" also contains a similar nonchalance and use of AAVE, as Solange brags to an unknown person:

> He think I don't want to tear it up
> We came all night long, won't you let it up?
> . . .
> Let's go, nobody givin', addressing me
> So nobody dress can effeminate me

Her threats could be to square up with someone or to invite them to a dance-off in the middle of the club floor;

it is for the listener to decide. As the song progresses, the instrumentals open up and a layer of vocalized "ehs" and "woahs" are looped to back up the beat. Over this patchwork rhythm, Solange erupts in what sounds like a freestyled verse declaring she's been "swangin' on them days." She elongates the line in a southern drawl and sounds more like Beyoncé than she ever has before. She is referencing the "swangas" used on cars in the Houston slab scene, but also, like Missy, uses AAVE and specifically African American references to connect directly with her audience. From this vantage point, it is easy to see Solange as a descendant of Missy's school of Black avant-garde production.

Another avant-garde influence on Solange is the minimalist composer Steve Reich, known for his use of sampling and process music (sounds that arise from a process of shifting or changing over time). Reich's explorations in classical arrangements are an early iteration of the sampling used in DJ culture that we know today. *Rolling Stone* once referred to him as the "father of sampling," noting that the use of Black voices (especially in his most famous pieces, 1968's "It's Gonna Rain" and 1989's "Come Out"), repetitive basslines, static sounds, and stretches of dead space is what also interests DJs today.[19] The French pianist, composer, and collaborator on this album, Christophe Chassol, was impressed by Solange's musical knowledge as the two spoke often about Reich's influence on her: "It was something she was really interested in from a point of view from an avant-garde sound that is Black American," says

Chassol. "It was really interesting to mix these concepts of music with Black American concepts."[20] Reich's influence can be heard throughout the record in its use of repetition and minimalism. The closing song, "I'm a Witness," is a perfect example of forming experimental sound—a throbbing sub bass that swells and shrinks dramatically as the song progresses—into a pop structure.

Chassol began working with Solange after he, accompanied by the drummer Jamire Williams—an old high school friend of Solange's—opened for her at Radio City Hall in 2017. Two months later, Chassol and Williams were in Solange's studio talking about her upbringing, her parents, the first time she met her husband and recording every word. It formed the basis of Chassol's contribution using speech harmonization, a technique in which a note is assigned for every syllable pronounced, creating melodies from everyday conversation. Solange's declaration of independence on "Can I Hold the Mic" is an example of this work. Her expansion of the r&b and pop structure into the realm of experimental composing has confused some listeners. The song that stirred up the most conversation was "Things I Imagined," a hazy two-minute composition of scattered jazz chords and frequently changing pitches and time signatures while Solange finds new ways to repeat "I saw things I imagined." Fans took to social media to declare their confusion, joking that lighting incense might help them understand the song's New Age vibes.

Solange was aware some fans might take a while to

adjust to her new sound. Whenever she doubted herself, she looked to women like Missy Elliott, Erykah Badu, Syreeta Wright, and Alice Coltrane and let their examples guide her: "I've learned so much from the work of all of these women. I also really connect with having to accept that their work is not and has not been for me, that it's for them! Before I put the album out I thought about the sort of divisiveness that it might bring, and many of these women helped me to feel assurance in standing firm in my expressions."[21] Chassol understood that Solange is not looking for anyone's approval: "She's not forced to make a hit. She doesn't have to. That's freedom."[22]

EPILOGUE

Solange never intended to record an album so soon after *A Seat at the Table*. She's known for taking her time between releases. She began writing songs out of a need to express the fear and uncertainty she felt during battles with her health. "I was going through a personal shift and evolution after years of being afraid of what I would hear if I really silenced myself," she told *The Face* in May 2019. "I think when I let go of that I knew exactly how the sonic language needed to be translated."[1] Making the album led Solange to the other side of an intensely dark period in her life and left her with a renewed sense of self. At an album listening party in Houston a few days after *When I Get Home*'s release, Solange was asked about being a Black woman today. Her answer couldn't be more euphoric: "I felt so much joy in this project. . . . To have something out in this world that feels like a true reflection of who I am, and the things that I love to listen to, the things that I love to experience, as a snapshot of myself at this present time. Any time you truly feel seen you feel a certain level of joy."[2]

With each project she releases, Solange proclaims that it is the true embodiment of herself. Each has represented a vital stage in her life that she felt called to document. *Solo Star* was her teenage fantasy of what life could be; *Sol-Angel and the Hadley St. Dreams*, her breakup album; *True*, her rebellious wandering in the desert; *A Seat at the Table*, her search for answers; and *When I Get Home*, her journey back to structure and belonging. Like a true artist, she knows there is not just one authentic depiction of your essence. Over time it changes, like a series of portraits taken over decades, but it still remains an honest depiction of you.

Today Solange breezes through the cultural landscape, inspiring everyone she meets. Her Saint Heron label released early music by both Kelela and Sampha, who are now stars in their own right. The guitarist Bryndon Cook met Solange on her 2013 tour while he was still a theater major. He went on to become her bandleader, has released music under the title Starchild and the New Romantic, and has been profiled in the *New York Times* and *Vogue*. Her unapologetic need to unravel Black identity and the political structures that surround it has influenced the music industry and other artists in her circle. For the writer Ally Hickson, *A Seat at the Table* reopened the possibility of being both politically honest and successful: "We had a time period when music was superficial, say, for talking about relationships. I feel like there are some artists who want to take chances now."[3] The journalist Natelegé Whaley sees the Bronx's own, rapper Cardi B, in the same light as Solange, explaining, "Cardi B is very outspoken, and she comes from a place where you have to be outspoken to survive. So now that she's got a microphone, she's like, hey, I'm not afraid, because that's what got me to where I am now."[4]

Solange's power can be heard in Donald Glover's 2018 damnation of Uncle Sam, "This Is America." It pours out of Chicago-based neo-soul star Jamila Woods, whose album *Legacy! Legacy!* (2019) is an ode to legendary artists of color, using their guidance to unpack what it means to live as a person of color. The contemporary artist who seems most aligned with Solange is the British experimental singer-songwriter FKA twigs. Solange and twigs have never worked together or mentioned each other's existence (except for twigs sharing a video of herself pole dancing to "Cranes in the Sky"). Twigs has also yet to make an outright political statement, preferring to let her art speak for her. Nevertheless, both artists have much in common. They cite Kate Bush and Aaliyah as equal influences in their work. They use visual media and contemporary dance as modes of expression when words will not suffice. Finally, they show a dedication to ensuring that the Black community's input in avant-garde art is recognized, carving out a space for themselves in an industry that often struggles to read their eccentricities.

Solange herself is still open to inspiration. Her adoration for Houston rapper Megan Thee Stallion, whose own form of Black high-femme sexuality is central to her work, has been well documented. On Instagram, Solange has filmed herself dancing as Megan performs inches away from her. On Twitter, she shared her favorite Megan lyrics and joined a thread praising Megan's skills. Her outpouring of love for artists like Megan has coincided with the rebirth of a more openly fun-loving Solange than we've ever seen before, via social media at least. At her current stage in life, Solange is a free-spirited woman who knows her own mind, knows her body, and has grown to accept the road she has to travel. Like many of us, she is aware that no good comes from using social media as a venting space for anger. Instead, she prefers visual media, tweeting pictures of a new design or sharing Instagram stories of her girls' trip with Kelela. She opened up to her fans on Twitter, following the *When I Get Home* release, answering questions about how the album was made and retweeting her fans' adoration for her work.

She even began to share her selfies and videos of herself taken during the moments when she was really feeling herself. Sharing a collection of video selfies, she tweeted: "No mo digital hoardingggg taking up spaceee i luh yallll."[5] No longer lingering on her phone, we can see Solange's personality hang out in all its goofy, sultry, thirst-trap-ready form. It speaks to the journey Solange has made as an artist and as a woman. She grew up in the spotlight, and using the women in her community as guiding lights, navigated herself around the numerous roadblocks that often stop Black female pop stars from embracing their glory. Fulfilling her dream of being truly independent after she left Geffen Records in 2009, exactly a decade prior to *When I Get Home*, Solange now answers to no one but herself.

BLACK WOMEN AGAINST THE WORLD

In June 2019, during her address to her fellow graduating seniors at the Rhode Island School of Design, the commencement speaker Qualeasha Wood paid homage to *When*

I Get Home's "Things I Imagined," explaining how the album changed her life: "When I arrived at RISD in September 2015, I too saw things I imagined. I saw the dreams of a little Black girl from New Jersey finally coming true." She pauses to breathe in deeply. She takes in the moment and readies herself to continue. "A little Black girl who never saw art in her future let alone [that it] would become her future. I saw my parents' dreams come true, and their parents', and their parents' too."[6] Solange reposted Wood's speech on her Instagram story, showing her appreciation for her Black female fans and their ability to use her music to manifest their dreams.

It is with the same spirit that I reflect on the sizable impact she has made on my life, work, and sense of self. Solange truly is the embodiment of Black girl freedom that Black women spend a lifetime striving to achieve. It is a freedom in which you can be the best version of yourself every day, one in which you can fully explore the deepest regions of your mind for your art, in which you are allowed to take the time and space needed to heal. It is a world I tried to bring into existence in my own life when I channeled Solange through my band's cover of "Cranes in the Sky." At first, the wandering bass line and unusual time signature threw us. Punks work best in 4/4. Once we brought the song down an octave and stuck with a more rigid version of Raphael Saadiq's glorious bass line, we were ready to go.

We set out to imbue the mournful song with even more

dirge and gloom to match how we interpreted it through our punk ears. We wanted to reference '90s stoner rock and the drone pop of bands like California's alt-rock group Mazzy Star. We slowed everything down to a glacial pace and kept the distortion on throughout, adding a whack of reverb toward the end. Ours is a somewhat dumbed-down version of the original. I only play two chords for the majority of the song and then launch into a lo-fi, reimagined version of the melody for my guitar solo. It is the highlight of the set every time we play. I always look at the audience's faces to see when they recognize the hook.

Though our version is simplistic, I feel it is reflective of my love for Solange and how I interpret her work. Her blissed-out funk pop keeps me buoyed during the highs (an all-Black female picnic I attended included Solange on our jubilant party playlist) and the lows (I blasted both *Lemonade* and *A Seat at the Table* after I broke up with my ex). I love her work, but I do not aim to copy her. Great artists never inspire mimicry. Instead, the hallmark of a truly inspiring artist is the ability to light the flame of creativity inside whoever takes them in. Like so many Black women, I took Solange into my heart and mixed her up with my punk-rock feminism and my '60s girl group devotion to contribute my own attempts at understanding the unwieldy beast that is music.

On stage, whenever my band plays, we stand in a line, as equals. Black women against the world, singing out to the back of the room and beyond, calling to the other Black punk girls out there. We ask them to join us in our choir that extends beyond the stage we stand on, singing about the realities and complexities of Black women's lives in all their glory. It is a vision I hope Solange would be proud of.

ACKNOWLEDGMENTS

In 2017, when I first learned that my proposal for this book had been accepted, my life and career were in remarkably different places. At the time, I was about to be made redundant from my job at a charity, my band was preparing to record its debut album with no label or industry support, and I was terrified of going out alone and creating a new path for myself. Back then, I struggled to find the confidence to position myself as an authoritative voice with the power to persuade others. Fortunately, my fears were assuaged by the many friends, family members, and colleagues in my life who helped steer me toward positivity, ensuring that neither I nor this project broke down.

First, I would like to thank series editor Evelyn McDonnell, who first suggested I put together a proposal for the Music Matters series after I wrote a selection of essays for her anthology *Women Who Rock: Bessie to Beyoncé. Girl Groups to Riot Grrrl.* She offered me intuitive guidance and demonstrated a steadfast belief in my ability to accomplish this project. Thanks also to my editor Casey Kittrell, who took a chance that this punk Solange fan could offer a unique take on the artist I admired so much. You were always patient and reminded me that my voice was as important as the story I was telling.

To the many people I interviewed for this project, thank

you for your time, experience, and insight; Olugbenga Adelekan, Ray Angry, Jessica Ashman, Carsten Schack, Christophe Chassol, Erin Christovale, Priya Elan, Janine Francois, Lakeisha Goedluck, Nadine Goepfert, Melissa Harris-Perry, Ally Hickson, Beverly Ishmael, Didi Jenning, Keith Murphy, Sean Nicholas Savage, Lance Scott Walker, Seher Sikandar, Gabrielle Smith, and Natelegé Whaley. I was unable to fit a few interviews into the book due to length and the project moving in a different direction from my original plan. Those interviews still helped shape the project massively, so I would like to thank those interviewees also.

My family's story features throughout my book, so I would like to thank all of the Phillips clan and the Browns, on my mum's side. Growing up around all of you kind and proud people made me into the person I am today. I would specifically like to thank my brother Chris, my mum Joan, and my dad Glen, whose story has been retold according to his recollection. My family loved, laughed, and resisted in the same ways many other Black British families have since we first came here. I hope this history is evident in their story.

I should also thank many people in the UK punk scene who, for better and worse, drove me to create spaces of my own, where the voices of punks of color could be centered and valued. A special shout-out to the Decolonise Fest collective and everyone who has ever attended the festival; you're all helping to build a more radical and inclusive music scene. Also, obviously so much love has to be devoted to my bandmates in Big Joanie, Estella Adeyeri and Chardine Taylor-Stone. Thanks for your unwavering support and belief in me. You both do such vital work in trade union organizing, LGBTQ+ activism, and supporting young women and girls in the music industry through initiatives like Girls Rock Camp, and I'm forever motivated by the dedication and passion you both show for your activism.

This book was written on the road with Big Joanie, balancing my laptop in bumpy tour vans, backstage at venues, and at Airbnbs across the world. Through this method of writing, I believe the book has a punk spirit embedded in its very DNA, so I guess I've got to thank the road and every person who ever came to a Big Joanie gig for this one, too. Thanks for giving me a reason to keep writing.

NOTES

1. Solange Takes Her Seat

1. Julianne Escobedo Shepherd, "Solange, *A Seat at the Table*," *Pitchfork*, October 5, 2016, pitchfork.com/reviews/albums/22482-a-seat-at-the -table/.

2. Top Arsenal, "Solange Knowles Tell[s] Childhood Stories in Talk about New Album," YouTube, March 4, 2019, youtube.com/watch?v=uJF -AEzvm_s&t=13s.

3. Robert Christgau, "Xgau Sez," Robertchristgau.com, December 4, 2018, robertchristgau.com/xgausez.php?d=2018-12-04.

4. Christgau, "Xgau Sez."

5. TMZ, "Beyoncé and Solange Are Just Like Michael and Janet!," YouTube, October 13, 2016; video has since been deleted.

6. Lakeisha Goedluck, author interview, phone, November 30, 2018.

7. Natelegé Whaley, author interview, phone, April 23, 2018.

8. Ayana Mathis, "Solange, the Polymathic Cultural Force," *New York Times Style Magazine*, October 15, 2018, web.archive.org/web /20200823005357/https://www.nytimes.com/2018/10/15/t-magazine /solange-interview.html.

9. Home Office, Aoife O'Neill, "Hate Crime, England and Wales, 2016/17," published October 17, 2017, assets.publishing.service.gov.uk /government/uploads/system/uploads/attachment_data/file/652136 /hate-crime-1617-hosb1717.pdf.

10. Lord Ashcroft, "How the United Kingdom Voted on Thursday . . . and Why," *Lord Ashcroft Polls*, June 24, 2016, lordashcroftpolls.com/2016/06 /how-the-united-kingdom-voted-and-why.

11. Jamie Grierson, "More Than Half of Young People in Jail Are of BME Background," *Guardian*, January 29, 2019, theguardian.com /society/2019/jan/29/more-than-half-young-people-jail-are-of-bme -background.

12. Debbie Weekes-Bernard, "Poverty and Ethnicity in the Labour

Market," Joseph Rowntree Foundation, September 29, 2017, jrf.org.uk
/report/poverty-ethnicity-labour-market.
13. Rhian Daly, "Solange Says She 'Broke Out of Hospital' to Perform at
Lovebox," *NME*, July 15, 2017, nme.com/news/music/solange-says
-broke-hospital-perform-lovebox-2111735#gMr0rQl1lK5XJ4vD.99.

2. Little Sister

1. BeyoncéWorld9481, "Mathew Knowles - My American Story,"
YouTube, uploaded February 1, 2011, youtube.com/watch?v=
7C4xSPGLNUA.
2. Emilia Petraca, "Solange Knowles Talks Music, Style Icons and Her
Upcoming Museum Tour," *W*, April 24, 2017, wmagazine.com/story
/solange-knowles-coachella-a-seat-at-the-table-museum-tour.
3. Reverie 2, "Blackstar Rising and the Purple Reign: Celebrating the
Legacies of David Bowie and Prince," YouTube, January 26, 2017;
youtube.com/watch?v=LSAspByaV78; link no longer works.
4. Solange Knowles, "Solange Wrote the Most Powerful Letter to Her
Teenage Self," *Teen Vogue*, May 17, 2017, teenvogue.com/story/solange
-knowles-letter-to-teenage-self-cover-story-music-issue.
5. Solange Knowles, "Solange Wrote the Most Powerful Letter."
6. Top Arsenal, "Solange Knowles Tell[s] Childhood Stories in Talk about
New Album," YouTube, March 4, 2019, youtube.com/watch?v=uJF
-AEzvm_s&t=13s.
7. Beyoncé Knowles, "Solange Brings It All Full Circle with Her Sister
Beyoncé," *Interview*, January 10, 2017, interviewmagazine.com/music
/solange#_.
8. Maria Shriver, "Architects of Change: Tina Knowles Lawson,"
Facebook, May 11, 2018, facebook.com/MariaShriver/videos
/10160829797655455/.
9. Andres Tardio, "Solange Mistakenly Goes Off on Reporter," Hip Hop
DX, August 28, 2008, hiphopdx.com/news/id.7601/title.solange
-knowles-mistakenly-goes-off-on-reporter.
10. Solange Knowles, "Solange Wrote the Most Powerful Letter."
11. Antwaun Sargent, "Solange Knowles Is Not a Pop Star," *Surface*,
January 11, 2018 (Jan./Feb. 2018 cover), surfacemag.com/articles
/solange-knowles-is-not-a-pop-star.

12. Doreen St. Félix, "Solange on New Music and Why She's 'Not Interested in Entertainment at This Moment,'" *Billboard*, March 1, 2018, billboard .com/articles/news/magazine-feature/8221722/solange-interview -billboard-cover-story-2018.

13. St. Félix, "Solange on New Music."

14. Anupa Mistry, "An Honest Conversation with Solange Knowles," *Fader*, September 30, 2016, thefader.com/2016/09/30/solange-knowles-a-seat -at-the-table-interview.

15. Beyoncé Knowles, "Solange Brings It All Full Circle."

16. Tavi Gevinson, "Exclusive: Solange Knowles in Conversation with Tavi Gevinson about "A Seat at the Table," *W*, September 30, 2016, wmagazine.com/story/exclusive-solange-knowles-in-conversation -with-tavi-gevinson-about-a-seat-at-the-table.

17. June Jordan, *Some of Us Did Not Die* (New York: Basic Books, 2003), 270–271.

18. bell hooks, *Sisters of the Yam: Black Women and Self-Recovery* (Cambridge, MA: South End Press, 2005), 111.

19. Tavi Gevinson, "Exclusive: Solange Knowles in Conversation."

20. Robert Stanton, "Two Houston Neighborhoods Called Most Dangerous in U.S.," *Houston Chronicle*, February 2, 2018, chron.com/business/real -estate/article/Two-Houston-neighborhoods-called-most-dangerous -4476367.php.

21. Reverie 2, "Blackstar Rising and the Purple Reign."

22 Beyoncé Knowles, "Solange Brings It All Full Circle."

23. *The Hot 97 Morning Show*, "Does Solange Think Nas Is Better Than Jay-Z???," YouTube, September 13, 2018, youtube.com/watch?v= BljaY1DU5vE.

3. The Making of a Solo Star

1. Reverie 2, "Blackstar Rising and the Purple Reign: Celebrating the Legacies of David Bowie and Prince," YouTube, January 26, 2017, youtube.com/watch?v=LSAspByaV78; link no longer works.

2. Sal Cinequemani, "Review: Solange, *Solo Star*," *Slant*, January 24, 2003, slantmagazine.com/music/solange-solo-star.

3. J. Victoria Sanders, "Solange: *Solo Star*," *Pop Matters*, June 8, 2003, popmatters.com/solange-solo-2496069193.html.

Notes

4. Corey Moss, "Solange, Beyoncé's Lil' Sis, Says She's No Destiny's Child," *MTV*, March 15, 2002, mtv.com/news/1452941/solange -Beyoncés-lil-sis-says-shes-no-destinys-child.

5. Essence.com interview, "Solange Knowles: Flying Solo," *Essence*, December 16, 2009, essence.com/news/solange-knowles-flying-solo.

6. Jeremy Allen, "20 Things You Didn't Know about Kate Bush's 'Wuthering Heights,'" *NME*, August 26, 2014, nme.com/blogs/nme -blogs/20-things-you-didnt-know-about-kate-bushs-wuthering -heights-766195.

7. Dads-Space interview, "Dads-Space.com: Exclusive Solange Video Interview Part 2," YouTube, June 11, 2009, youtube.com/watch?v= hHyqjQGvdjQ.

8. Dads-Space interview.

9. United States Census Bureau, "Moscow City, Idaho," April 1, 2010, census.gov/quickfacts/fact/table/moscowcityidaho/LND110210.

10. Jim Meehan, "Destiny Brought Smith to UI," *Spokesman Review*, September 23, 2005, spokesman.com/stories/2005/sep/23/destiny -brought-smith-to-ui.

11. Salamishah Tillet, "Solange Is the Superstar We Need Now," *Elle*, February 9, 2017, elle.com/culture/celebrities/news/a42830/solange -knowles-march-2017-cover.

12. Solange Knowles, Twitter, July 15, 2017, twitter.com/solangeknowles /status/886407810384355328.

13. Carsten Schack, author interview, email, June 19, 2018.

14. Carsten Schack, author interview, email, June 19, 2018.

15. Priya Elan, "Solange: *Sol-Angel and the Hadley St Dreams*," *Times*, August 15, 2008, web.archive.org/web/20110616202605/http:// entertainment.timesonline.co.uk/tol/arts_and_entertainment/music/cd _reviews/article4532014.ece.

16. Priya Elan, author interview, phone, November 29, 2018.

17. Keith Murphy, author interview, phone, November 29, 2018.

18. Solange Knowles Q&A, *Cosmo Girl*, August 25, 2008, web.archive.org /web/20090810190126/http://www.cosmogirl.com/blog/solange -knowles-qa.

19. Tim Finney, "Solange: *Sol-Angel and the Hadley St. Dreams*," *Pitchfork*, September 18, 2008, pitchfork.com/reviews/albums/12203-sol-angel -and-the-hadley-st-dreams.

20. Keith Murphy, "Forget Her Sister: The Outspoken Solange Created One of the Year's Best R&B Albums," *Vibe*, November 2008, 87.
21. Keith Murphy, author interview, phone, November 29, 2018.
22. Reverie 2, "Blackstar Rising and the Purple Reign."
23. HoneyMagazine, "Estelle and Solange Interview Backstage," YouTube, April 3, 2009, youtube.com/watch?v=Nwf4yxmzJsk.
24. Judnick Mayard, "A Seat with Us: A Conversation between Solange Knowles, Mrs. Tina Lawson, and Judnick Mayard," Saint Heron, September 30, 2016, web.archive.org/web/20171109201932/http://saintheron.com/featured/a-seat-with-us-a-conversation-between-solange-knowles-mrs-tina-lawson-judnick-mayard.
25. Melissa Bradshaw, "'Imagery, and a Little Bit of Satire': An Interview with Frank Ocean," *The Quietus*, November 22, 2011, thequietus.com/articles/07450-frank-ocean-interview.
26. Briana Younger, "Black Musicians on Being Boxed in by R&B and Rap Expectations: 'We Fit in So Many Things,'" *Pitchfork*, September 28, 2017, pitchfork.com/thepitch/Black-musicians-on-being-boxed-in-by-randb-and-rap-expectations-we-fit-in-so-many-things.

4. Bite the Hand, It Never Fed You

1. Keith Murphy, "A Long Convo with . . . Solange," *Vibe*, July 1, 2010, vibe.com/2010/07/long-convo-solange.
2. BrooklynVegan, "Jay-Z Gives Grizzly Bear Props on Fuse (after MSG Show)," YouTube, September 11, 2009, youtube.com/watch?v=VHpf6cGFmLo.
3. Brittany Spanos, "The Joy of Lizzo," *Rolling Stone*, January 22, 2020, rollingstone.com/music/music-features/lizzo-cover-story-interview-truth-hurts-grammys-937009.
4. Andrew Perry, "Vampire Weekend Interview," *Telegraph*, March 31, 2010, telegraph.co.uk/culture/music/rockandpopfeatures/7541984/Vampire-Weekend-interview.html.
5. Ben Beaumont-Thomas, "Vampire Weekend's Ezra Koenig: 'Rock Music Is Dead, so It's More Joyful to Me,'" *Guardian*, June 27, 2019, theguardian.com/music/2019/jun/27/vampire-weekend-ezra-koenig-who-knows-when-youll-turn-a-corner-and-feel-really-happy.
6. Zach Kelly, "Solange: 'Stillness Is the Move' (Dirty Projectors Cover),"

Pitchfork, November 24, 2009, pitchfork.com/reviews/tracks/11645
-stillness-is-the-move-dirty-projectors-cover.

7. Kiss FM (UK), "Solange Knowles Talks 'Losing You,' Relationship
   and More," YouTube, January 18, 2013, youtube.com/watch?v=
   xjidBDalxFs.

8. Stephen Doig, "Meet the Dandies of Brazzaville," *Telegraph*, January
   13, 2014, telegraph.co.uk/men/fashion-and-style/10564648/Meet-the
   -dandies-of-Brazzaville.html.

9. The World Bank, "The World Bank in the Republic of Congo," October
   21, 2019, worldbank.org/en/country/congo/overview.

10. Matthew Schnipper, "Interview: Solange," *Fader*, October 2, 2012,
    thefader.com/2012/10/02/interview-solange.

11. Schnipper, "Interview: Solange."

12. Africa Is a Country, "Township Life Has Never Looked so Glam,"
    October 5, 2012, africasacountry.com/2012/10/when-solange-filmed
    -a-music-video-in-a-cape-town-township.

13. Randall Roberts, "Review: Solange Stays 'True' to the Beat," *Los
    Angeles Times*, January 8, 2013, latimes.com/entertainment/music/la
    -xpm-2013-jan-08-la-et-ms-solange-ture-review-20130108-story.html.

14. Nick Levine, "Solange Knowles *True* Review," BBC Music, 2013, bbc.co
    .uk/music/reviews/w3d3.

15. Murphy, "A Long Convo with . . . Solange."

16. Stelios Phili, "Q&A: Solange Knowles on Why Working with Kevin
    Barnes 'Makes All the Fucking Sense in the World,'" *Village Voice*, May
    25, 2010, villagevoice.com/2010/05/25/qa-solange-knowles-on-why
    -working-with-kevin-barnes-makes-all-the-fucking-sense-in-the-world.

17. Phili, "Q&A: Solange Knowles."

18. Hot 97, "Does Solange Think Nas Is Better Than Jay-Z???," YouTube,
    September 19, 2013, youtube.com/watch?v=BljaY1DU5vE&t=265s.

19. Dayo Olopade, "The Rise of the Black Hipster," *The Root*, May 19, 2009,
    theroot.com/the-rise-of-the-black-hipster-1790869385.

20. Eric Harvey, "I Started a Joke: 'PBR&B;' and What Genres Mean
    Now," *Pitchfork*, October 7, 2013, pitchfork.com/thepitch/95-i-started
    -a-joke-pbrb-and-what-genres-mean-now.

21. Carrie Battan, "Solange: *True*," *Pitchfork*, November 28, 2012, pitchfork
    .com/reviews/albums/17373-true/.

22. Harriet Gibsone, "Solange Knowles Reportedly Falls Out with 'Wizard' Producer Dev Hynes," *Guardian*, November 25, 2013, theguardian.com /music/2013/nov/25/solange-dev-hynes-twitter-feud-Beyoncé.

23. Phili, "Q&A: Solange Knowles."

24. Phili, "Q&A: Solange Knowles."

25. *New York Times*, Popcast, November 1, 2013, podcasts.nytimes.com /podcasts/2013/01/11/arts/music/11popcast_pod/0111-popcast.mp3.

26. Judnick Mayard, "A Seat with Us: A Conversation between Solange Knowles, Mrs. Tina Lawson, and Judnick Mayard," Saint Heron, September 30, 2016, web.archive.org/web/20171109201932/http:// saintheron.com/featured/a-seat-with-us-a-conversation-between -solange-knowles-mrs-tina-lawson-judnick-mayard.

5. Rooting for Everybody Black

1. Ray Angry, author interview, phone, September 25, 2018.

2 Olugbenga Adelekan, author interview, phone, November 23, 2018.

3. Olugbenga Adelekan, author interview, phone, November 23, 2018.

4. Olugbenga Adelekan, author interview, phone, November 23, 2018.

5. Olugbenga Adelekan, author interview, phone, November 23, 2018.

6. Anupa Mistry, "An Honest Conversation with Solange Knowles," *Fader*, September 30, 2016, thefader.com/2016/09/30/solange-knowles-a-seat -at-the-table-interview.

7. Mistry, "An Honest Conversation."

8. Solange Knowles, *A Seat at the Table*, LP, Saint Records, 2016.

9. *Variety*, "Issa Rae - 'I'm rooting for everybody Black' - Full Emmys Red Carpet Interview," YouTube, September 19, 2017, youtube.com/watch ?v=WafoKj6MzcU.

10. Ari Shapiro, "'We've Always Had a Seat at the Table': Solange on Conversations That Heal," *All Things Considered*, NPR, November 11, 2016, npr.org/2016/11/11/501165834/weve-always-had-a-seat-at-the -table-solange-on-conversations-that-heal.

11. bed wench, Twitter, December 1, 2018, twitter.com/lareinanegraa /status/1069072623240441856.

12. Carol Frohlinger, "Sheryl Sandberg on Why Women Need to 'Sit at the Table,'" *Forbes*, January 18, 2011, forbes.com/sites/work-in-progress

/2011/01/18/sheryl-sandberg-on-why-women-need-to-sit-at-the
-table/#5dd6efbf6de9.

13. Melissa Harris-Perry, author interview, phone, April 26, 2018.

14. Harriet Staff, "Alexis Pauline Gumbs Talks about Kitchen Table: Women of Color Press," Poetry Foundation, June 13, 2012, poetryfoundation.org/harriet/2012/06/alexis-pauline-gumbs-talks -about-kitchen-table-women-of-color-press.

15. Nina Simone, "Nina Simone: An Artist's Duty," YouTube, February 21, 2013, youtube.com/watch?v=99V0mMNf5fo.

16. Molly Fischer, "The Great Awokening: What Happens to Culture in an Era of Identity Politics?," *The Cut*, January 8, 2018, thecut.com/2018/01 /pop-cultures-great-awokening.html.

17. Solange Knowles, "And Do You Belong? I Do," Saint Heron, web .archive.org/web/20200509131841/https://saintheron.com/and-do -you-belong-i-do.

18. Sean Nicholas Savage, author interview, phone, October 21, 2018.

6. Creating Community

1. Reni Eddo-Lodge, *Why I'm No Longer Talking to White People about Race* (London: Bloomsbury, 2017), 154–155.

2. bell hooks, *Sisters of the Yam: Black Women and Self-Recovery* (Cambridge: South End Press), 122.

3. hooks, *Sisters of the Yam*, 122.

4. I sent out a call on Twitter asking for interviewees for *Why Solange Matters*. Separately, I also directly contacted Black female journalists who reviewed *A Seat at the Table*. Most of the interviewees were either in the music industry, in the media industry, or were community organizers.

5. Ally Hickson, author interview, phone, December 8, 2018.

6. Didi Jenning, author interview, phone, April 15, 2018.

7. Janine Francois, author interview, phone, January 7, 2019.

8. Jessica Ashman, author interview, phone, May 15, 2018.

9. Gabrielle Smith, author interview, phone, November 26, 2018.

10. Janine Francois, author interview, phone, January 7, 2019.

11. Seher Sikandar, *Testimonies from the Table* (Self-published), May 17, 2017.

12. Sikandar, *Testimonies from the Table*.

13. Seher Sikandar, author interview, phone, May 2018.

14. Melissa Harris-Perry, author interview, Skype, April 26, 2018.

15. Melissa Harris-Perry, author interview, Skype, April 26, 2018.

16. Beyoncé Knowles, "Solange Brings It All Full Circle with Her Sister Beyoncé," *Interview*, January 10, 2017, interviewmagazine.com/music /solange#.

17. Donna McConnell, "Beyoncé's Solange Knowles Does a Britney . . . as She Shaves Off Her Locks," *Mail Online*, July 23, 2009, dailymail.co.uk /tvshowbiz/article-1201574/Beyoncés-sister-Solange-Knowles-does -Britney--singer-shaves-brunette-locks.html.

18. Dodai Stewart, "Solange Chops Hair, Is Called 'Insane,'" *Jezebel*, July 24, 2009, jezebel.com/solange-chops-hair-is-called-insane-5322008.

19. Stewart, "Solange Chops Hair."

20. Beyoncé Knowles, "Solange Brings It All Full Circle."

21. Morgan Jerkins, "Solange's New Album Is Not for Everyone," *Elle*, October 3, 2016, elle.com/culture/music/a39712/solange-seat-table.

22. Angelica Bastien, "Solange Knowles on Family, Body Politics and Her Move into Art," *ES*, October 18, 2017, standard.co.uk/lifestyle /esmagazine/solange-knowles-on-family-body-politics-and-her-move -into-art-a3659816.html.

23. Ruth McKee, "Evening Standard Sorry for Airbrushing Out Solange Knowles' Braids," *Guardian*, October 21, 2017, theguardian.com/music /2017/oct/21/evening-standard-sorry-for-airbrushing-out-solange -knowles-braids.

24. Song Exploder, "Episode 94: Solange, 'Cranes in the Sky,'" January 16, 2017, songexploder.net/solange.

25. Beyoncé Knowles, "Solange Brings It All Full Circle."

26. Nadine Goepfert, author interview, phone, August 6, 2018.

27. Nadine Goepfert, author interview, phone, August 6, 2018.

28. Antwaun Sargent, "Solange Knowles Is Not a Pop Star," *Surface*, January 11, 2018, surfacemag.com/articles/solange-knowles-is-not -a-pop-star.

29. "Harnessing the Power of the 'Angry Black Woman,'" *All Things Considered*, NPR, February 24, 2019, npr.org/2019/02/24/689925868 /harnessing-the-power-of-the-angry-black-woman.

30. GordanGlobe, "Maya Angelou on the Difference in Use and Power of Anger and Bitterness," YouTube, August 17, 2017, youtube.com/watch ?v=b6N47Y0vbLg.

31. Billy Nilles, "Beyoncé, Jay-Z and Solange Step in an Elevator and the Rest Is History: Remembering That Infamous Met Gala Moment 5 Years Later," *E! News*, May 4, 2019, eonline.com/uk/news/1038196/beyonce -jay-z-and-solange-step-in-an-elevator-and-the-rest-is-history -remembering-that-infamous-met-gala-moment-5-years-later.

32. Polly Vernon, "'I Didn't Like Being a Celebrity. It's a Service Job. Like Washing Toilets,'" *Observer*, July 7, 2007, theguardian.com/music/2007 /jul/08/popandrock2.

33. Race Disparity Audit, gov.uk, October 10, 2017, gov.uk/government /publications/race-disparity-audit.

34. Krim K. Lacey, Regina Parnell, Dawne M. Mouzon, et al., "The Mental Health of US Black Women: The Roles of Social Context and Severe Intimate Partner Violence," *BMJ Open*, October 19, 2015, bmjopen.bmj .com/content/5/10/e008415.info.

35. Audre Lorde, *A Burst of Light: Essays* (Ithaca, NY: Firebrand Books, 1988), 130.

36. Jennifer C. Nash, "Practicing Love: Black Feminism, Love-Politics, and Post-Intersectionality," *Meridians* 11, no. 2 (2011): 3.

37. Sarah Mirk, "Audre Lorde Thought of Self-Care as an 'Act of Political Warfare,'" *Bitch Media*, February 18, 2016, bitchmedia.org/article /audre-lorde-thought-self-care-act-political-warfare.

38. Combahee River Collective, "The Combahee River Collective Statement," In *Home Girls: A Black Feminist Anthology*, ed. Barbara Smith (New York: Kitchen Table Press, 1983), 4.

39. Earl Sweatshirt, "Stay Inside with Earl Sweatshirt and Solange Knowles," Red Bull Radio, September 30, 2018, youtube.com/watch ?v=c_bePy5Y8q4.

40. Susan Rosenberg, "Set and Reset: Trisha Brown's Postmodern Masterpiece," *BAMorg*, YouTube, January 22, 2016, youtube.com /watch?v=4juID0hSyaw.

41. Sargent, "Solange Knowles Is Not a Pop Star."

42. Sargent, "Solange Knowles Is Not a Pop Star."

43. Anni Ferguson, "'The Lowest of the Stack': Why Black Women

Are Struggling with Mental Health," *Guardian*, February 8, 2016, theguardian.com/lifeandstyle/2016/feb/08/black-women-mental -health-high-rates-depression-anxiety.

7. For Us, By Us

1. Herbert G. Ruffin II, "Black Lives Matter: The Growth of a New Social Justice Movement," *Black Past*, August 23, 2015, Blackpast .org/african-american-history/Black-lives-matter-growth-new-social -justice-movement.

2. Christina Coleman (@ChrissyCole) "I got a chance to lend a hand to the #BKLYN4Trayvon rally. @Solangeknowles Thank you for reminding our bros & sisters that we have voices," Twitter, July 15, 2013, twitter .com/ChrissyCole/status/356782261703680001.

3. Jennifer Pearson, "'I'm for truth. . . I'm for justice': Beyoncé's Sister Solange Knowles Quotes Malcolm X as She Leads Rally in Protest of Zimmerman Not Guilty Verdict," *Daily Mail*, July 15, 2013, dailymail .co.uk/tvshowbiz/article-2363892/Beyoncés-sister-Solange-Knowles -quotes-Malcom-X-leads-rally-protest-Zimmerman-guilty-verdict .html.

4. Judnick Mayard, "A Seat with Us: A Conversation between Solange Knowles, Mrs. Tina Lawson, and Judnick Mayard," *Saint Heron*, web .archive.org/web/20171114154604/http://saintheron.com/featured /a-seat-with-us-a-conversation-between-solange-knowles-mrs-tina -lawson-judnick-mayard.

5. James Grebey, "Solange Debuts 'Rise,' a Powerful New Song 'for Ferguson, for Baltimore,'" *Spin*, May 15, 2015, spin.com/2015/05 /solange-rise-new-song-ferguson-baltimore.

6. Ari Shapiro, "'We've Always Had a Seat at the Table': Solange on Conversations That Heal," *All Things Considered*, NPR, November 11, 2016, npr.org/2016/11/11/501165834/weve-always-had-a-seat-at-the -table-solange-on-conversations-that-heal.

7. Claudia Jones's *Caribbean Carnival Souvenir* program, 1960, British Library, bl.uk/collection-items/claudia-jones-caribbean-carnival -souvenir-programme-1960.

8. Reverie 2, "Blackstar Rising and the Purple Reign: Celebrating the

Legacies of David Bowie and Prince," YouTube, January 26, 2017, youtube.com/watch?v=LSAspByaV78; link no longer works.

9. Mayard, "A Seat with Us."

10. Aaron Ross Coleman, "Black Capitalism Won't Save Us," *The Nation*, May 22, 2019, thenation.com/article/archive/nipsey-killer-mike-race -economics.

11. Shapiro, "'We've Always Had a Seat at the Table.'"

12. Anupa Mistry, "An Honest Conversation with Solange Knowles," *Fader*, September 30, 2016, thefader.com/2016/09/30/solange-knowles-a-seat -at-the-table-interview.

13. The Bluegrass Professors, "James Baldwin: How Much Time Do You Want for Your 'Progress'?" YouTube, May 22, 2016, youtube.com /watch?v=UBFDdTIYZ6Q.

14. Marie Solis, "When Dismantling Power Dismantles You Instead," *Vice*, December 7, 2018, vice.com/en_us/article/3k95kk/when-dismantling -power-dismantles-you-instead-v25n4.

15. Solis, "When Dismantling Power Dismantles You Instead."

16. Tavi Gevinson, "Exclusive: Solange Knowles in Conversation with Tavi Gevinson about "A Seat at the Table," *W*, September 30, 2016, wmagazine.com/story/exclusive-solange-knowles-in-conversation -with-tavi-gevinson-about-a-seat-at-the-table.

17. Didi Jenning, author interview, Skype, April 15, 2018.

18. Didi Jenning, author interview, Skype, April 15, 2018.

19. Beverly Ishmael, author interview, phone, May 17, 2018.

20. Jessica Ashman, author interview, London, May 15, 2018.

8. When I Get Home

1. Sarah Lindig, "Beyoncé and Tina Lawson Showed Up to Support Solange during Her SNL Debut," *Harper's Bazaar*, November 6, 2016, harpersbazaar.com/culture/film-tv/al8683/solange-knowles-snl -Beyoncé-mom.

2. Soulhead, "Black Star Rising and the Purple Reign Yale 1 26 17 Solange Interview p3," YouTube, December 21, 2017, youtube.com/watch?v= vso42d5fN0E&t=26s.

3. Doreen St. Félix, "Solange on New Music and Why She's 'Not Interested

in Entertainment at This Moment,'" *Billboard*, March 1, 2018, billboard
.com/articles/news/magazine-feature/8221722/solange-interview
-billboard-cover-story-2018.

4. Lynette Nylander, "The Full Story: Solange Knowles for AnOther
Magazine A/W17," *AnOther*, September 13, 2017, anothermag.com
/fashion-beauty/10141/the-full-story-solange-knowles-for-another
-magazine-a-w17.

5. Ikea, "GÅTFULL – IKEA and Saint Heron to Explore What Matters
in the Disruptive Home," June 4, 2019, newsroom.inter.ikea.com
/news/g-tfull---ikea-and-saint-heron-to-explore-what-matters-in-the
-disruptive-home/s/2a25318c-ea22-47b7-a954-b3d49f4d74f9.

6. Sol LeWitt, "Sentences on Conceptual Art," *0 to 9* (New York), 1969,
altx.com/vizarts/conceptual.html.

7. Erin Christovale, author interview, phone, December 4, 2018.

8. Brittany Spanos, "Solange Dominates Space, Tears Down Walls at
Masterful Guggenheim Show," *Rolling Stone*, May 19, 2017, rollingstone
.com/music/music-live-reviews/solange-dominates-space-tears-down
-walls-at-masterful-guggenheim-show-112885.

9. St. Félix, "Solange on New Music."

10. St. Félix, "Solange on New Music."

11. Ayana Mathis, "Solange, the Polymathic Cultural Force," *New
York Times Style Magazine*, October 15, 2018, web.archive.org/web
/20200823005357/https://www.nytimes.com/2018/10/15/t-magazine
/solange-interview.html.

12. Zora Neale Hurston, "Characteristics in Negro Expression," in *Negro:
An Anthology*, ed. Nancy Cunard (London: Hours Press, 1934), 24.

13. Top Arsenal, "Solange Knowles Tell[s] Childhood Stories in Talk about
New Album," YouTube, March 4, 2019, youtube.com/watch?v=uJF
-AEzvm_s&t=13s.

14. Michelle Kim, "How Solange and Mitski Reconsider Who Can Be the
Cowboy," *Pitchfork*, March 21, 2019, pitchfork.com/thepitch/how
-solange-and-mitski-reconsider-who-can-be-the-cowboy.

15. Jesse Serwer, "DJ Screw: From Cough Syrup to Full-Blown Fever,"
Guardian, November 11, 2010, theguardian.com/music/2010/nov/11/dj
-screw-drake-fever-ray.

16. WePresent, "Solange Knowles: When I Get Home," *WePresent*, July

26, 2019, wepresent.wetransfer.com/story/solange-knowles-when-i-get
-home.

17. Lance Scott Walker, author interview, email, May 6, 2019.

18. Lance Scott Walker, author interview, email, May 6, 2019.

19. Heidi Sherman, "The Father of Sampling Speaks: Steve Reich
    Discusses His Influence on DJ Culture," *Rolling Stone*, March 27, 1999,
    rollingstone.com/music/music-news/the-father-of-sampling-speaks
    -122357.

20. Christophe Chassol, author interview, phone, November 27, 2018.

21. Brooke McCord and Grace Wales Bonner, "Grace Wales Bonner in
    Conversation with Solange," *The Face*, May 30, 2019, theface.com/music
    /solange-grace-wales-bonner-devotional-sound-1.

22. Elias Leight, "How (and Why) Solange Channeled Stevie Wonder,
    Devin the Dude and D'Angelo on Her New Album," *Rolling Stone*,
    March 6, 2019, rollingstone.com/music/music-features/making-of
    -solange-when-i-get-home-801973.

Epilogue

1. Brooke McCord and Grace Wales Bonner, "Grace Wales Bonner in
   Conversation with Solange," *The Face*, May 30, 2019, theface.com
   /music/solange-grace-wales-bonner-devotional-sound-1.

2. Top Arsenal, "Solange Knowles Tell[s] Childhood Stories in Talk
   about New Album," YouTube, March 4, 2019, youtube.com/watch?v=
   uJF-AEzvm_s&t=13s. https://i-d.vice.com/en_uk/article/3kgpw8
   /solange-knowles-interview-tim-walker.

3. Ally Hickson, author interview, phone, December 8, 2018.

4. Natelegé Whaley, author interview, phone, April 23, 2018.

5. Solangeknowles, Twitter, March 25, 2019, twitter.com/solangeknowles
   /status/1110033784131342337.

6. godisablckwxmn, Twitter, June 2, 2019, twitter.com/godisaBlackwxmn
   /status/1135008951689515009.